W9-DCE-866

Translated Texts for Historians

This series is designed to meet the needs both of students of ancient and medieval history and of others who wish to broaden their study by reading source material, but whose knowledge of Latin or Greek is not sufficient to allow them to do so in the original language. Many important Late Imperial and Dark Age texts are currently unavailable in translation, and it is hoped that TTH will help fill this gap and complement the secondary literature in English which already exists. The series relates principally to the period 300-800 AD and will include Late Imperial, Greek, Byzantine and Syriac texts as well as source books illustrating a particular period or theme. Each volume is a self-contained scholarly translation with an introductory essay on the text and its author, and notes indicating major problems of interpretation, including textual difficulties.

Cover illustration: Procession of Martyrs Mosaic. Sant'Appollinare Nuevo, Ravenna.

Already published

Latin Series I
Gregory of Tours: Life of the Fathers
Translated with an introduction by EDWARD JAMES
164 pp., 1985 (reprinted 1986), ISBN 0 85323 115 X

Latin Series II
Pacatus: Panegyric to the Emperor Theodosius
Translated with an introduction by C.E.V. NIXON
128 pp., 1987, ISBN 0 85323 076 5

Greek Series I
The Emperor Julian: Panegyric and Polemic
Claudius Mamertinus, John Chrysostom,
Ephrem the Syrian
Edited by SAMUEL N.C. LIEU
160 pp., 1986, ISBN 0 85323 335 7

Forthcoming

Gregory of Tours: Glory of the Confessors
Translated with an introduction by RAYMOND VAN DAM
Approx. 150 pp., Autumn 1988, ISBN 0 85323 226 1

Liber Pontificalis
Translated with an introduction by RAYMOND DAVIS
Approx. 150 pp., Autumn 1988, ISBN 0 85323 216 4

Translated Texts for Historians
Latin Series III

Gregory of Tours
Glory of the Martyrs

Translated with an introduction by
RAYMOND VAN DAM

Liverpool
University
Press

First published 1988 by
Liverpool University Press
PO Box 147, Liverpool L69 3BX

British Library Cataloguing-in-Publication Data

Gregory, *Saint*, Bishop of Tours.
   The glory of martyrs.
   1. Saints - Biographies - Early works
   I. Title II. Series
   270
   ISBN 0 85323 236 9

Printed in Great Britain by
Oxford University Press Printing House

CONTENTS

PREFACE

Gregory of Tours was always thankful for the assistance of his patron saints; modern scholars are equally grateful for the support of institutions and the advice of friends and colleagues. A Fellowship from the National Endowment for the Humanities made it possible for me to consider translating both Gregory's *Glory of the martyrs* (in this volume) and his *Glory of the confessors* (in a companion volume). The National Humanities Center then provided me with an unrivaled atmosphere of serenity and encouragement. The University of Michigan now offers access to a computer and laser printer. Gillian Clark, Christa Mee, and Ian Wood have commented on the introduction, translation, and notes and on their presentation in the series "Translated Texts for Historians". Gregory would have understood how much appreciation lies behind even a short list of *capitula* such as this one.

University of Michigan
May 1988

ABBREVIATIONS

ACW   Ancient Christian Writers (Westminster).

BAR   British Archaeological Reports (Oxford).

CChrL   *Corpus Christianorum*, series latina (Turnhout).

CSEL   *Corpus scriptorum ecclesisticorum latinorum* (Vienna).

GCS   *Die griechischen christlichen Schriftsteller der ersten Jahrhunderte* (Berlin).

LCL   Loeb Classical Library (Cambridge, Massachusetts, and London).

MGH   *Monumenta Germaniae historica* (Berlin, Hannover, and Leipzig).

     AA   Auctores antiquissimi.

     SRM   Scriptores rerum merovingicarum.

NPNF   A select library of Nicene and Post-Nicene Fathers of the Christian Church, 2nd series (reprinted Grand Rapids).

PL   *Patrologia latina* (Paris); and Supplementa, ed. A. Hamman (Paris, 1958-1974).

PLRE   *The prosopography of the later Roman empire.* Vol. 2, ed. J.R.Martindale (Cambridge, 1980).

Writings of Gregory of Tours:

GC   *Glory of the confessors*

GM   *Glory of the martyrs*

HF   *Histories* ["History of the Franks"]

VJ   *Suffering and miracles of the martyr St Julian*

VM   *Miracles of the bishop St Martin*

VP   *Life of the fathers*

INTRODUCTION

In 573 Gregory became bishop of Tours. This promotion was not unexpected, because since the early sixth century several of his ancestors had served as bishops throughout central and southern Gaul. Gregory himself was born in the late 530s and grew up in Clermont, where Gallus, his father's brother, was bishop. During his episcopacy Gallus enhanced the cult of St Julian by instituting an annual pilgrimage to the saint's shrine at Brioude, another town in the Auvergne. Gregory's entire family was specially attached to the cult of St Julian, and Gregory eventually considered himself a "foster son" of the saint whom he thought of as his "special patron". Gregory's family also had distinctive connections with Tours and its cult of St Martin. In 563 Gregory completed a difficult pilgrimage to the tomb of St Martin in his church outside Tours, where the saint cured him of a severe fever. By then Tours had become virtually a family see. The current bishop was a cousin of Gregory's mother, and after Gregory succeeded him, he could boast that all but five of his predecessors had been members of his family. During the last twenty years of his life until his death (probably) in 594, Gregory was therefore maintaining both the family's prominence in the ecclesiastical hierarchy and its consequential links with Tours and the cult of St Martin.[1]

Service in the ecclesiastical hierarchy, however, only added to the family's local influence. One of Gregory's grandfathers had still claimed the rank of senator, a prestigious title that revived memories of five centuries of Roman rule in Gaul. But by the later fifth century the Roman empire had already vanished from most of Gaul as various barbarian leaders had gradually established small kingdoms. The most successful had been Clovis, who had first ruthlessly made himself king of all the Franks in northern Gaul. His most significant military

---

[1] L.Pietri (1983) 247-64, and Van Dam (1985) 202-17, provide details about Gregory and his family; important introductory surveys to Gregory and his writings include Krusch (1951), Buchner (1955), and Vollmann (1983).

success had been his victory in 507 over the Visigoths, who consequently abandoned most of their possessions in southern and central Gaul and moved into Spain. At some point during his reign Clovis also astutely converted to orthodox catholic Christianity. Much of Roman Gaul had already been converted to catholic Christianity during the previous century. By the time of his death in 511, Clovis had therefore consolidated the rule of the Franks over much of Gaul and had earned the loyalty of many catholic bishops and their Roman congregations.[2]

As Gregory grew to adulthood in the middle of the sixth century this kingdom of the Franks sometimes looked to be on the verge of disintegration. All legitimate sons of the ruling Merovingian family expected to receive portions of the kingdom to rule as their own minikingdoms. These mini-kingdoms generally had territorial cores, but they also often included control over individual cities scattered around Gaul. Usually several kings were ruling concurrently; Gregory had to deal with sons, grandsons, and great-grandsons of Clovis. Usually too these various kings were feuding with each other and sometimes making war on each other.

Wars were in fact perhaps the primary emphasis of Gregory's writings, and they included not only the wars of kings with their enemies, but also the wars of martyrs with pagans and of the catholic churches with heretics [HF I praef.]. During his tenure as bishop of Tours Gregory wrote several works about the wars of kings, saints, and churchmen. Near the end of his career he listed his important works [HF X.31]: "I have written ten books of histories, seven books of miracles, and one book about the life of the fathers. I wrote one volume of commentary on the book of Psalms and one book about the liturgical offices of the church."[3] He also translated an account of the

---

[2] Three excellent and concise introductory discussions of early medieval Gaul are Wallace-Hadrill (1967), James (1982), and Geary (1988); Wood (1985) presents a thorough re-examination of Clovis' conversion.

[3] Gregory's title for his book on the liturgical offices was somewhat misleading, since the treatise contained first a section describing seven man-made wonders of the world and seven natural wonders, and then a section describing the movement of the stars that was intended to enable men to celebrate liturgical offices at the appropriate hours during the night: ed. B.Krusch, *MGH*, SRM 1.2 (1885) 857-72; first section trans. McDermott (1975) 209-18.

Seven Sleepers in Ephesus [cf. *GM* 94], wrote a preface for a collection of liturgical masses [*HF* II.22], and condensed a book about the miracles of St Andrew [cf. *GM* 30]. With the exception of his commentary on the Psalms, of which only the introduction, a table of contents, and a few fragments are extant,[4] and his preface for the book of masses, his important literary works have survived. His ten books of histories, now commonly (although misleadingly) known as the "History of the Franks" [*HF*], are certainly the most familiar to modern readers, in part because they provide the most detailed continuous narrative of events in sixth-century Gaul, in part too because they have been well translated into English (and other modern languages).[5]

In contrast, Gregory's seven books of miracles and one book on the life of the fathers are much less familiar to modern readers. When Gregory listed these books again in the preface to one of them, he counted them as eight books of miracles [*GC* praef.], which is how modern scholars now also customarily consider them. In Gregory's own sequence these eight books included:

1. one book entitled "The glory of the martyrs" [*GM*], consisting of stories about martyrs and the miracles they or their relics performed;

2. one book entitled "The suffering and miracles of the martyr St Julian" [*VJ*], consisting of stories about the saint and his shrine at Brioude;

3-6. four books entitled "The miracles of the bishop St Martin" [*VM* 1-4], consisting of stories about the patron saint of Tours and the miracles he performed, primarily at Tours, before and during Gregory's episcopacy;[6]

7. one book entitled "The life of the fathers" [*VP*], consisting of a series of short biographies of illustrious men and women in

[4] Ed. B.Krusch, *MGH*, SRM 1.2 (1885) 874-7.
[5] The best editions are by W.Arndt, *MGH*, SRM 1.1 (1885), and by B.Krusch and W.Levison, *MGH*, SRM 1.1 (1937-1951); Goffart (1987), is an important clarification of title and textual history. The most accessible English translations are Dalton (1927) and Thorpe (1974).
[6] McDermott (1975) 129-95, includes translations of *VM* 1, *VP* 6-7, and the prefaces to all the books of miracles. Since Gregory once begged that his books be kept intact [*HF* X.31], he would perhaps not have approved of only selections in translation.

4 INTRODUCTION

the church, almost all of whom lived during the sixth century
and among whom were some of Gregory's own relatives;[7] and

8. one book entitled "The glory of the confessors" [GC], consisting
of stories about confessors and the miracles they or their relics
performed.[8]

Only some of these books have been translated into English; this
volume is the first complete translation into English of "The glory of
the martyrs."

Gregory wrote most, if not all, of his surviving works during the
years of his episcopacy. He seems to have composed his book about
the glory of the martyrs during his final decade. In the book he
mentioned his previous book about the miracles of St Julian [GM 64],
in the final chapter of which [VJ 50] he had referred to his life of bishop
Nicetius of Lyon, in which in turn he had mentioned a military expedition that took place in 585 [VP 8.11, with HF VII.35-8]. Since
Gregory mentioned the same expedition in GM 104, and since he noted
as deceased a bishop who had died in 585 [GM 33, with HF VIII.22,
IX.33], he was most likely still writing his book about the martyrs
after 585. In another story [GM 5] he stressed that then Radegund had
been still alive; this emphasis suggests that Gregory was presumably
also still writing his book about the martyrs after her death in 587. He
had, however, apparently completed it by the early 590s when he
included a cross reference to it in a chapter of his final book of histories
[HF X.24, with GM 95]. Perhaps he had completed the book, or at
least a first draft of it, already by 588, since he listed it in the preface to
his book about the glory of the confessors [GC praef.]; he seems to
have been working on this book about the confessors during 587 and
588, since in it he described a man who became a bishop in 588 as still
a royal secretary [GC 93, with HF IX.23]. Although these various
cross references and internal allusions therefore suggest that Gregory
composed his book about the glory of the martyrs between 585 and
588, hesitation is still recommended, because Gregory was constantly
revising his writings over the years. The preface to his book about the
miracles of the confessors, for instance, was perhaps a later addition, or

[7] Translated by James (1985), with introduction and notes.
[8] Translated by Van Dam (forthcoming), with introduction and notes.

at least included later rewriting. Furthermore, if the deacon who provided the story about his return from Rome [*GM* 82] is to be identified with the deacon who was in Rome for the accession of pope Gregory I in 590 and who also was an informant of Gregory of Tours [cf. *HF* X.1], and if the eastern bishop who visited Tours in 591 told Gregory about the martyrs of Armenia [*GM* 95], then he was still writing or revising at least various chapters of his book about the glory of the martyrs into the early 590s.[9]

The haphazard nature of Gregory's composition has left its mark on the arrangement of the chapters in this book. An underlying structured organization is not readily apparent, and the book anyway admitted many digressions. The opening chapters were about the "martyr" who had conclusively defined the subsequent paradigm of martyrdom: Jesus Christ. Relics from his passion were some of the most prized in the Mediterranean world, and the longest chapter in the book described the power of fragments of the True Cross and the nails used to affix Jesus to the cross [*GM* 5]. Subsequent chapters discussed the people who had been closest to Jesus, among them the Virgin Mary (whose inclusion in a book about martyrs may seem peculiar), John the Baptist, and some of the original apostles. These initial chapters also demonstrate Gregory's readiness to switch back and forth between places and times, since in them he indiscriminately mixed stories about the Jordan River and eastern cities with stories about miracles that he had personally witnessed in Gaul and notable contemporary shrines in Spain. The common link in these stories was some connection to the particular saints or their relics. Surprisingly, only after he had completed more than a quarter of the book did Gregory finally include an account of the deacon Stephen. Many Christians had considered Stephen to be the protomartyr; Gregory did describe Stephen as the first martyr at Jerusalem [*GM* 33], but he minimized his paradigmatic significance by introducing him so late in his book.

After concentrating on these Eastern martyrs Gregory turned to Western martyrs. He first mentioned martyrs at Rome and Italy, perhaps because some of the earliest Christian communities had been

---

[9] For arguments about the dates of composition of the various books of miracles, see Monod (1872) 41-5, who dates the *GM* to c.586-587, and especially Krusch (1885) 451-6, who stresses Gregory's frequent revisions.

established there and because he still thought of Rome as "the city of cities, the great head of the whole world" [*HF* V praef.; cf. *GM* 82]. But having once started with Rome, he also mentioned a bishop who had become a martyr in 526 during the reign of king Theodoric of the Ostrogoths [*GM* 39]. Finally, almost halfway through his book, Gregory began to discuss Gallic martyrs. The first Gallic martyrs he mentioned were also some of the earliest, although it is not clear that Gregory was always aware of or concerned about chronology. These early martyrs included the forty-eight martyrs of Lyon from the later second century [*GM* 48] and some of the more or less apocryphal missionaries sent to Gaul in the middle of the third century. Gregory then adopted, rather indiscriminately, a loose chronological and geographical pattern; reference to an early martyr at a Gallic city could be followed by reference to a much later martyr at the same city [e.g. *GM* 56-57]. Gregory once stressed that in Gaul many had been "crowned with the celestial jewels of martyrdom" [*HF* I.28]. In fact, since persecutions, and therefore the opportunity for actual martyrdom, were unlikely in Gregory's Gaul, most of the martyrs he mentioned had lived either much earlier or outside Gaul. But because most of the miracles that happened at their shrines in Gaul were contemporary ones, Gregory was always switching back and forth between past and present, and between Gaul and elsewhere.

Near the end of the book Gregory included another series of stories about foreign martyrs and their shrines in Spain, Italy, North Africa, and regions in the eastern empire. These stories seem to have represented either a digression or an afterthought, since Gregory eventually decided to "return to the martyrs of Gaul" [*GM* 103]. But however often Gregory added or revised, he preserved a symmetry between the beginning and the end of the book. Gregory had started the book by stressing the impressive miracles performed by Jesus Christ and his relics, in particular the relics of the True Cross. He ended it by emphasizing the power of the sign of the cross that people could use even to shoo away a pesky fly [*GM* 106].

Gregory's book about the glory of the martyrs highlights both his strengths and his weaknesses as an historian of past events and a chronicler of contemporary events. Stories about saints, their relics, and their miracles naturally raise suspicions in modern historians, in part because some of the stories referred to events that had happened centuries earlier or in remote regions, in part too because most modern historians are uncertain how to deal with reports of miracles. Neither scruple bothered Gregory. His concern for simply preserving the stories took priority over any worries about their veracity: "it was surely improper that these miracles disappear from memory" [GC praef.]. For information about both past and contemporary people and events he relied upon, and usually accepted with great trust, both written documents and oral traditions: "some events are guaranteed by the account of Scripture, others are established by the testimony of other writers, and still others are accepted on the authority of personal observation" [VP 17 praef.].

For very early events the most important written sources were books included in the New Testament, in particular the Gospels and the Acts of the Apostles. For events from the history of the early church Gregory referred to, and sometimes seems even to have read, the "histories of the suffering" of various martyrs [GM 31, 34, 35, 37, 46, 50, 56, 57, 63, 70, 73, 104]; claimed to have used the historical account of Eusebius of Caesarea, although certainly in the Latin translation made by Rufinus [GM 20]; and paraphrased poems by the early fifth-century bishop Paulinus of Nola [GM 103]. For events in the post-Constantinian church, Gregory used the poems of the later, fourth-century bishop Damasus of Rome [GM 37] and his younger contemporary Prudentius [GM 40, 42, 90, 92, 105], and an account of the Seven Sleepers at Ephesus that he himself translated into Latin [GM 94]. In addition to these written sources that he specifically cited Gregory no doubt also used others, although it is often difficult to track them down.

Gregory was usually imprecise about the oral sources he used for past events, even though he recorded many ancient traditions. Occasionally he mentioned some unspecified "believers" from Italy [GM 39, 43], or an anonymous man whose story had supplemented a written account [GM 46]. Often he introduced various traditions or stories with formulaic phrases, "some say", "they claim", "it is widely said." Sometimes he simply dispensed with these vague verifying references: "I have heard about something that happened years ago in Gaul" [GM 105]. Modern historians, in consequence, tend to be suspicious about most of these traditions, especially when they are as inherently implausible as the stories about the woman from Bazas who was present at the execution of John the Baptist and collected some of his blood [*GM* 11], and the woman from Saint-Jean-de-Maurienne who acquired the thumb of John the Baptist at Jerusalem [*GM* 13]. These traditions seem more likely to have originated as later etiological legends that explained the presence and potency of various relics in Gaul or that provided substance to fill out the careers of martyrs whose historical existence is dubious.

In the face of difficulties in collecting any information about early centuries Gregory made a credible effort that deserves respect. Yet because of the importance of Gregory's writings as historical sources, modern historians now have difficulty transcending his limitations. Gregory may have begun his book about martyrs with stories about Jesus Christ, the founder of Christianity, as well as about other early saints in the East, but he offered little information about the history of early Christianity in Gaul. Modern historians too cannot therefore write a satisfactory history of early Christianity in Gaul. They can discuss some isolated events such as the persecution at Lyon in 177 that is independently documented (but barely mentioned by Gregory: see *GM* 48), but otherwise they must wait for the careers of Hilary of Poitiers and Martin of Tours during the middle fourth century for adequate documentation. Gregory's anecdotes are significant as evidence for what he and his contemporaries believed about the early church in Gaul, but his information becomes historically reliable only for the late Roman and, especially, the sixth-century church.[10]

For these more contemporary events Gregory again used some written documents. They included a poem by his friend Fortunatus [*GM* 41] and perhaps a record of a miracle composed by bishop Bertramn of Bordeaux [*GM* 33]. The most important sources of information about contemporary miracles, however, were oral reports and conversations. For events that happened outside Gaul Gregory's informants included a deacon named Johannes who had visited Bethlehem and the Jordan River [*GM* 1, 18, 87]; "many people" who had all visited the Jordan River [*GM* 20]; an unnamed man who had visited Jerusalem [*GM* 5]; a priest who had visited the island of Chios [*GM* 101]; a man

---

[10] The best surveys of the history of the church in Gaul are Griffe (1964-1966), who covers the Roman period through the fifth century, and Wallace-Hadrill (1983), who covers the Frankish period; see also the relevant sections in Baus, Beck, Ewig and Vogt (1980).

named Theodorus who had visited India [*GM* 31]; and various people who had been cured by the power of saints in the East [*GM* 97]. Gregory received information about Italy from a deacon who had visited Rome [*GM* 82] and another man [*GM* 41], and about Spain from a man who knew a cleric there [*GM* 81]. Within Gaul itself Gregory talked with many people. Among them were churchmen such as bishop Avitus of Clermont [*GM* 66], an unnamed abbot [*GM* 5], a priest who had visited Lake Leman [*GM* 75], and his friend abbot Aredius [*GM* 36, 41]. He also received information from Radegund, the former queen who went to live in the convent she had founded at Poitiers [*GM* 5], Fedamius and Epyrechius, otherwise unknown men [*GM* 52, 53], and his mother and his sister [*GM* 50, 70, 83, 85]. These were the only informants whom Gregory specifically mentioned, although he surely had others. For some contemporary events outside and within Gaul Gregory did not specify his informants and instead introduced stories with formulaic phrases such as "I heard", "some say", "it is popularly claimed."[11]

Contemporary miracle stories are important evidence for the nature of Christianity in sixth-century Gaul and have been used as such by modern historians. Gregory's references to events and people outside Gaul are equally telling evidence for the extent of contact between Gaul and the old Roman world. In this book about martyrs Gregory made no reference to Britain. This omission is not surprising, since the invasions of the Angles and Saxons had isolated Britain from the continent and Gregory rarely mentioned Britain in his other writings. He mentioned only one martyr in North Africa [*GM* 93]. But he mentioned several martyrs in both Spain and Italy. This emphasis on the two southern neighbors of Gaul is also not unexpected, since the Visigoths in Spain and the Ostrogoths, Byzantines, and Lombards in succession in Italy had constant dealings with the Franks.

Gregory's martyr stories also looked farther east, however, and they therefore raise again the long-standing question of the extent of interaction between East and West during the sixth century. Gregory mentioned shrines in Greece, Asia Minor, Syria, and Palestine (but not, significantly, in Egypt), as well as further east in Mesopotamia and

---

[11] For discussion of Gregory's sources and his reliability as an historian, see Kurth (1919) II:117-206.

India. Some of his information about events at these shrines from the remote past had come from written sources, although their reliability and accuracy are sometimes suspect. For contemporary events in the East he probably relied entirely upon oral accounts. During the sixth century men still travelled across the Mediterranean, whether as merchants, pilgrims, or diplomatic envoys [GM 30]. But the sum total of Gregory's knowledge about the eastern Mediterranean world of the later sixth century was remarkably slight, based mostly on hearsay and oral reports. It is unlikely that Gregory used any written accounts, even for the stories he included about contemporaries such as the emperor Justinian I, who reigned in Constantinople from 527 to 565, and his successor, Justin II, who reigned until 578 [GM 5, 102].[12]

Like his other writings, Gregory's book about the martyrs emphasized Gaul and the Gallic church; the relics of saints from elsewhere took on immediate significance usually only after they had arrived in Gaul and worked miracles there. Furthermore, and again like his other writings, this book also included Gregory's own personal experiences. Since these experiences covered most of his life, they allow modern historians to add texture to his life and career. When he was a young man, his mother gave him some relics that his father had once carried; although these relics were able to work miracles, neither his parents nor Gregory knew the names of the saints whose relics they were [GM 83]. Another time during his youth he and his mother attended a mass in honor of St Polycarp that was being celebrated in a village near Clermont [GM 85]. He also visited an oratory dedicated to the Virgin Mary that was near Clermont [GM 8] and carried a reliquary in the shape of a cross that contained relics of the Virgin Mary and St Martin [GM 10]. At Dijon St Benignus cured his infected eyes [GM 50], and at Poitiers he visited the tomb of St Hilary and the convent of Radegund [GM 5]. Other episodes probably happened during his years

---

[12] Baynes (1929) 231-3, emphasizes Gregory's limited knowledge of eastern affairs. In contrast, Cameron (1975) points out the similarities of Gregory's assessments of Justin II and Tiberius II in the *HF* to those of such contemporary Eastern historians as Evagrius and John of Ephesus and suggests that Gregory possibly used a written chronicle; but she does not discuss the *GM* or any of the other books of miracles. Ewig (1960) and (1964) presents the evidence for the cults of eastern and other non-Gallic saints in Gaul.

as bishop of Tours. There he dedicated one oratory with relics of John the Baptist and another with relics of St Stephen [*GM* 14, 33], watched men commit perjury in a church dedicated to the Virgin Mary and John the Baptist [*GM* 19], fell asleep during vigils on Christmas Eve [*GM* 86], and saw soldiers who had been stricken with illnesses because of their disrespect for St Vincentius [*GM* 104]. At some time he acquired a silk robe that had once been wrapped around the True Cross at Jerusalem [*GM* 5], and he saw samples of the fine wool produced by trees near Jericho [*GM* 17]. These experiences indicate that Gregory shared with other Christians in Gaul a high regard for the efficacy of saints and relics; they also demonstrate that he enjoyed a special relationship with many saints in addition to St Martin and St Julian. In fact, elsewhere Gregory mentioned that his father's family claimed descent from one of the martyrs at Lyon [*VP* 6.1]. Gregory was no doubt one of the few Gauls who could therefore complement his friendships with various martyr saints with direct descent from a prominent Gallic martyr.

Why did Gregory write his book about the glory of the martyrs? He seems to have had several purposes in mind, most of which derived from his personal theology and beliefs. In this book Gregory promoted a theology of the significance of martyrdom that also had practical implications for ordinary believers.[13] Initially martyrs had been the people who had simply "witnessed" or seen Jesus Christ in person; but as the early church had expanded, martyrs became exclusively those people who had witnessed to the tenacity of their belief in Jesus Christ by being executed for it, usually at the hands of civil magistrates. Most of the martyrs whom Gregory mentioned in the *GM* qualified under one of these criteria and some under both, such as the original apostles who had been the disciples of Jesus and who, according to later apocryphal traditions, had also suffered death for their commitment. But seeing Jesus in person had soon become no longer possible, and in later sixth-century Gaul execution for religious beliefs was no longer likely. Yet Gregory stressed that the paradigm of martyrdom remained

---

[13] Delehaye (1927) 74-121, discusses the development of the term "martyr"; Frend (1965), is a comprehensive survey of martyrdom and persecution through the fourth century.

relevant. Martyrdom had involved a "struggle" or "contest" in which men and women had competed as "athletes of Christ" [*GM* 52, 53, 72, 103]. This contest included suffering and perhaps even torture, but not necessarily immediate death. In this sense Jesus himself had set the example by suffering on the cross, but then rising from the dead. Other "martyrs" such as the Virgin Mary had been translated body and soul to Paradise [*GM* 4], or, like the evangelist John, had been buried in a tomb while still alive [*GM* 29]. Physical death was no longer a necessary component of martyrdom, and Gregory preferred to stress that martyrs were still "alive" in heaven: "although buried, the martyr lives in glory" [*GM* 56].

For rather than seeing it as an opportunity for individual heroism, Gregory consistently placed martyrdom in the context of the ecclesiastical community. "The glory of the martyrs" was equivalent to that "edification" of the church that Gregory had stressed at the outset was the proper topic of this book [*GM* praef., 30]. This edification implied the building up of Christianity and its influence in Gaul. More concretely, it also implied the necessity of constructing churches and shrines. Gregory lovingly documented the construction of monuments throughout Gaul as visible symbols of the heights to which catholic Christianity should aspire. He also recorded with great satisfaction the misfortune that befell an impious man who had the audacity to lower a tall church that blocked his view [*GM* 91].

This particular theological perspective on martyrdom had immediate implications for ordinary believers. One was that the martyrs, because they were still alive in heaven, were also available as mediators for ordinary believers. In Roman and Frankish society men were deeply dependent upon the patronage of their superiors, and the most successful men were those who had cultivated wide networks of friends, patrons, and supporters. Gregory transposed this hierarchy of informal connections to the court of heaven. Martyrs' miracles proved that they were "friends of God" [*GM* 63] who could therefore ensure his divinely majestic protection for their "foster children". At the moment of the final judgement, men could be confident that the martyrs whom they had venerated would act as their effective advocates before God [*GM* 106].

A second implication posed a more demanding application. Having imitated the example of Jesus, the martyrs now made that exalted paradigm of suffering more accessible by serving as exemplars for ordinary believers [*GM* 53]. Since martyrdom implied struggling and perhaps suffering but not necessarily dying, ordinary believers could demonstrate their own commitment by living virtuously. Gregory may have thought that the civil wars between Frankish kings caused more havoc and suffering than "in the time of the persecution of the emperor Diocletian' [*HF* IV.47]. But because the Frankish kings had accepted catholic Christianity, they did not in fact offer the opportunity for actual martyrdom by persecuting their subjects, as some pagan Roman emperors had once done in the remote past. Yet Gregory now held out the opportunity for even ordinary believers to become martyrs in the context of a moral struggle: "by resisting vices you will be considered a martyr" [*GM* 106]. People could make themselves into their own persecutors by suppressing their vices, and thus could become martyrs [*VP* 7 praef.]. Actual death had once been an irrevocable "confession" that had earned the gifts of salvation [*GM* 82]; moral resistance could now have the same effect. A man could make himself into a "martyr" in the sense of "a witness to the name of the Lord" [*GM* 50] through an exemplary life, and not necessarily a flamboyant death.

Gregory's reevaluation of martyrdom has hence transposed it from the context of persecution by godless rulers to the level of daily moral struggle. Once men had been persecuted because of the "name" of Christianity; Gregory now transformed that name into a rallying cry of exhortation: "There is great value in the name Christian, if you perform in deeds what you confess in faith" [*GM* 40]. Although some of Gregory's stories turned into didactic homilies that condemned greed, lust, and arrogance [*GM* 104], he always emphasized actual behavior over abstract recommendations. In these stories people could hear precisely how they were to live out the instructions of the Bible: "what the Lord said in the Gospel was fulfilled in this woman" [*GM* 13].

Gregory's book about martyrs also had another theological purpose that in a roundabout way he derived from his emphasis on martyrdom. Although persecution of catholic Christians was unlikely in Frankish Gaul, it did happen in some neighboring barbarian kingdoms. Throughout most of the sixth century the Visigoths in Spain continued to accept an Arian version of Christianity whose theology essentially subordinated the Son and the Holy Spirit to God the Father. Occasionally the Arian Visigothic kings persecuted catholic Christians in their kingdom [*GM* 81]. But Gregory was less interested in the opportunity for martyrdom through dying that they offered, than in

refuting their Arianism. In his books of histories he had included
accounts of debates he had had with representatives of Arianism [*HF*
V.43, VI.40]. In this book about the martyrs he inserted some chapters
that never mentioned martyrs or martyrdom but that did refute
Arianism, this time not by logical arguments but by the power of relics
[*GM* 12, 24-25] or by direct trials of strength [*GM* 79-80]. In one way
or another, Gregory intended to stress the inadequacies of Arianism: "the
power of the Lord destroys and disorders his enemies" [*GM* 25].

Gregory's arguments against Arianism in his books of histories
demonstrate that systematic theology was not one of his strengths [cf.
HF I praef., III praef.]. In contrast, the miracle stories in this book
about martyrs demonstrate that storytelling was one of his great talents.
For all their simplicity and occasional inconsistencies, these stories are
wonderfully forceful and vivid. Many of the anecdotes more closely
resemble scenes from drama than the dispassionate narrative perhaps
anticipated of an historian. In his stories Gregory included direct dialogues between participants, pointed exhortations to readers or listeners,
and descriptions of the emotional responses of the audiences present at
the original events that may have served as verbal cues for the responses
of audiences listening to a retelling: at the end of one story, "a great fear
arose in everyone, and no one again dared to tamper with the sacred
relics" [*GM* 13]. Another of his stories, although essentially irrelevant
to the theme of martyrs, still concisely captured Gregory's tendency to
transform the conflict between catholic Christianity and heretical
Arianism into a good yarn. The contortions of two opposing priests
struggling not to eat food blessed by the other was similar to a farcical
comedy of manners that ended with the Arian priest scalding his throat
and dying with a loud belch [*GM* 79]. Gregory, and perhaps his audiences too, seem to have found more insights in anecdotes than in
systematic theology; whatever the doctrinal subtleties, most people
could immediately understand how Arianism was the religious
equivalent of a bad case of indigestion.[14]

The dramatic quality of many of the stories suggests that Gregory
probably also had pastoral, liturgical, and devotional purposes in mind

---

[14] Auerbach (1953) 77-95, is such a wonderfully sensitive and perceptive
appreciation that it seems quite proper to have included Gregory in the same
book with Homer, Dante, Shakespeare, and Cervantes.

when he composed this book about the glory of the martyrs. During the celebration of saints' festivals readings from accounts of their lives or sufferings would be inserted into the liturgy [*GM* 85]. In the case of the martyr saints, these readings might well have emphasized their horrible sufferings that later congregations could reflect upon to stimulate their own resolve and to reassure themselves of their own ultimate redemption.[15] But because Gregory preferred to stress the moral rather than the physical dimension of suffering, some of his own stories may have been used as readings during the liturgy, either as replacements for existing histories or as substitutes for unavailable accounts [*GM* 40, 46, 103, for stories as *lectiones*]. Other stories were perhaps parts of sermons that Gregory had delivered as commentaries on readings from the histories of martyr saints or as exhortations to moral goodness that had nothing to do with martyrs [cf. *GM* 69].[16] Most people would therefore have heard, rather than read, these stories; for modern readers to catch their full flavor, they are best read aloud.

Although Gregory's Latin is usually straightforwardly comprehensible, it also poses many difficulties. Some of the difficulties are due to his style. Gregory tended to be verbose and sometimes lost the pacing and logic of a story or even of a sentence by multiplying subordinate clauses and digressions and by relying on passive verbs, abstract nouns, and clusters of synonyms. His style and manner of presentation often seem closer to the sweeping flow and colloquialism of a sermon or oral discourse than to the concentrated precision of a rewritten narrative. Other difficulties are due to Gregory's inadequate command of Latin. He himself admitted that he did not fully understand the subtleties of Latin syntax and that his prose made him look like a "lumbering ox" [*GC* praef.]. In its failure to understand nuances and details a translation faces the same accusation. But Gregory already provided a defense for both his own writings and subsequent transla-

---

[15] Brown (1981) 79-85, is a suggestive discussion of the complementary notions of disintegration and reintegration that people might reflect upon while hearing about the sufferings of martyrs.

[16] Note Bonnet (1890) 10 n.1, on *GM* 105-106: "ne seraient-ce pas là des morceaux de ses sermons, que le bon évêque aurait trouvés dignes de passer à la postérité?"

tions. For him, truth was found in deeds and not in the words that he admitted he was not skilled at manipulating [*GM* 80]. Modern readers of Gregory too, rather than faulting him for mistakes and obscurities, should instead be grateful for the copious and remarkable information he has provided about late Roman and early Merovingian Gallic society and in particular its contemporary cults of saints. Since the notes are meant merely to provide essential information, identifications, and cross-references to Gregory's other writings, and since in consideration of the potential readership they refer primarily to books and articles written in English or French, they can only hint at the possibilities for subsequent research that Gregory's books of miracles offer.

This translation is based on the great edition of Gregory's books of miracles published by Bruno Krusch in 1885. Previous editions had included one by Thierry Ruinart published in 1699, that was reprinted in *Patrologia Latina* vol.71, col.705-800. In 1857 H.L.Bordier published a text and a French translation of the whole of the *GM*. Modern scholars still rightly use both Ruinart's edition in *PL* and Bordier's text and translation; but it is important to note that the numbering of the chapters in these earlier editions of the *GM* differs from that in the edition by Krusch, which this translation follows. One obvious consequence that readers should additionally note is that modern scholars who do not use Krusch's edition will refer in their own books and articles to chapter numbers in the *GM* that differ from those here. The one change from Krusch's edition has to do with the *capitula*. Gregory provided a list of "headings" for each of his books. Rather than list them as Gregory (and Krusch) did as a table of contents, this translation has included them as introductory headings for each chapter.

Krusch was one of the great scholars of Frankish Gaul, and his editions of the writings of Gregory were a monumental achievement. In 1890 Max Bonnet published a book on Gregory's Latin that is still an essential commentary both on Gregory's writings and on Krusch's edition. In 1920 Krusch collated additional manuscripts that included various readings for the *GM* that are better or more sensible that those in his original edition and that this translation has therefore occasionally used. Although between 1937 and 1951 Krusch and W. Levison published a new edition of the *HF*, there has been little work on the text of the *GM* since Krusch's edition. A new, properly collated and edited text of all of Gregory's "Books of Miracles" would be most useful; equipped with a translation and a detailed linguistic and historical commentary in the manner of many of the wonderful editions in the series "Sources Chrétiennes", it would be indispensable.

TRANSLATION

Here begins the first book of miracles [entitled] "The glory of the blessed martyrs," written by Georgius Florentius Gregorius, bishop of Tours.

The priest Jerome, an important teacher of the church second [only] to the apostle Paul, relates that he was once led before the tribunal of the eternal Judge. Although stretched out in supplication, he was strongly criticized because he had too often read the subtleties of Cicero and the lies of Virgil; and in the presence of the holy angels he confessed to the Lord of all that he would never again read these books and that he would think only about whatever was judged worthy of God and advantageous to the edification of the church.[1] So also the apostle Paul

---

[1] In 374 Jerome's anxieties over how to reconcile his training in classical culture with a Christian austerity that was suspicious of secular literature had climaxed in this famous dream that he later described in a letter: see Jerome, *Ep.*22.30, ed. and trans. F.A.Wright, LCL (1933) 124-9, with Kelly (1975) 41-4. Copies of Jerome's letter were quickly available in Gaul: see Sulpicius Severus, *Dialogi* I.9.2, ed. C.Halm, *CSEL* 1 (1866) 160, and trans. A.Roberts, NPNF 2nd series, 11 (reprinted 1973) 28. For later Christians the dream became a paradigmatic account of the endless confrontation between sophisticated classical culture and plain Christianity: see Antin (1963), and Rice (1985). Note, however, that Gregory's own literary concern was the opposite of Jerome's. Despite his pedantic listing of classical gods and heroes, Gregory usually worried about the inadequacies of his style and syntax [*HF* I praef., *GC* praef.]. In fact, he once had his own dream in which he candidly admitted his deficiencies: "Is it not obvious to you that I am untrained in culture and that I do not dare to publicize such marvelous miracles because I am ignorant and uneducated?" [*VM* 1 praef.]. Gregory's self-assessment was quite accurate, because his familiarity with classical authors and Latin grammar was limited: see Bonnet (1890) 48-53, 76-80, Kurth (1919) I:1-29, and especially Riché (1976) 177-210, for the wider context of the survival of classical culture in southern and central Gaul. Yet with the encouragement of his mother, who pointed out that at least people could understand him [*VM* 1 praef.], Gregory continued to write in support of Christianity, not least because the gods of the pagan Roman pantheon were still

says: "Let us pursue what makes for peace and let us mutually preserve what makes for edification" [Romans 14:19]. And again: "Let no evil talk come from your mouth, but only whatever is good for edification, that it may give grace to those who hear" [Ephesians 4:29].

Hence it is proper for me to follow this advice by writing and proclaiming what edifies the church of God and what enriches barren minds to recognition of perfect faith by means of holy teaching. For it is not proper either to recall deceitful myths or to follow the wisdom of philosophers that is hostile to God, lest we slip into the penalty of eternal death when the Lord passes judgement. I am afraid of this result. And since I desire to publicize some of the miracles of saints that have until now been hidden, I do not wish myself to be overcome by or entangled in these snares. I do not commemorate the flight of Saturn, the wrath of Juno, the debaucheries of Jupiter, the insult of Neptune, the scepter of Aeolus, or the wars, shipwreck, and kingdoms of Aeneas. I say nothing about the mission of Cupid, the love for Ascanius and the wedding, tears, and fearsome destruction of Dido, the gloomy entrance court of Pluto, the debauched rape of Persephone, or the triple heads of Cerberus; nor will I repeat the conversations of Anchises, the trickeries of the man [Odysseus] from Ithaca, the cunning of Achilles, or the deceptions of Sinon. I will not recount the advice of Laocoon, the strength of Amphitryon's son [Hercules], or the contests, exiles, and fatal death of Janus.[2] I will not describe the shapes of the Eumenides or of different monsters, nor the contrivances of the other myths that this author [Virgil] has either deceitfully fabricated or depicted in heroic verse.

After noting that all these examples are, as it were, built on sand and soon to topple [cf. Matthew 7:26], let me turn instead to the divine miracles of the Gospels. Thus the evangelist John began [his Gospel] by saying: "In the beginning was the Word, and the Word was with

---

attractive to Franks and others [cf. *HF* II.29, VIII.15, *VP* 17.5]: see James (1982) 93-101, and Wallace-Hadrill (1983) 18-19, 33-5.

[2] Because Krusch (1885) 488 n.15, noted that nothing is known about the death of Janus, Bonnet (1890) 81 n.4, proposed Cacus, which McDermott (1975) 131, translated. Krusch himself suggested Turnus, and later collated a manuscript supporting his conjecture: see Krusch (1920) 712, 726. All of Gregory's allusions in this paragraph are to stories in Virgil's *Aeneid*: see Garrod (1919).

God, and the Word was God. He was in the beginning with God. All
things were made through him, and without him was nothing made"
[John 1:1-3]. Next he says: "And the Word was made flesh and dwelt
among us, and we have seen his glory, glory as if of the only begotten
from the Father; [the Word was] filled with grace and truth" [John
1:14]. But because he would be born in Bethlehem, the prophet says
this: "And you, Bethlehem Ephrathah, you are not the least among the
thousands of Judah. For from you a king will come forward who will
rule my people of Israel" [Micah 5:2]. That Nathanael from Cana in
Galilee also said this: "Rabbi, you are the Son of God. You are the
King of Israel" [John 1:49]. He is also the salvation of the world, concerning whom Simeon said: "Lord, now send your servant away in
peace, because my eyes have seen your salvation" [Luke 2:29-30].

1. The birth of our Lord Jesus Christ in Bethlehem.
    When therefore our Lord Jesus Christ was born according to the
flesh in the town of Bethlehem during the days of king Herod, according
to the account of the Gospels wise men came from the East to
Jerusalem and said: "Where is he who has been born King of the Jews?
For we have seen his star in the East and we have come to worship
him" [Matthew 2:2], and so forth.
    Indeed, there is in Bethlehem a large well from which the glorious
Mary is said to have drawn water. Often a famous miracle is demonstrated to onlookers: that is, the star that appeared to the wise men is
there revealed to the pure in heart. The pious cover their heads with
linen cloths, and come and lean over the mouth of the well. Then the
man whose merit will have prevailed sees the star move from one wall
of the well over the waters to the opposite wall in the same way as
stars are customarily moved above the orbit of the heavens. And
although many look, such a miracle is seen only by those whose mind
is more blameless. I have met some people who claimed that they had
seen the star. Recently however my deacon reported that he, with five
other men, had looked, but the star had appeared only to two of them.

2. The miracles of our Lord and Saviour.
    So our Lord Jesus Christ, in the flesh assumed from the Virgin,
deigned to show many miracles to people. For he converted drinking
water into the flavor of wine, he bestowed light upon the eyes of the
blind by chasing away night, he restored the mobility of paralytics by

removing their lameness, he extinguished the fevers of the ill by dispelling their burning heat, he healed a dropsical man by alleviating his tumor, he commanded leprosy to depart by the power of his holy kiss, and in a crowd of hostile Jews he liberated a woman under the control of a demon; he even walked upon the waves without the waters splitting apart,[3] and he removed the flow [of blood] from a woman who touched the saving fringe [of his garment]. He also performed many other miracles that the sacred history of the evangelists records. But although he restored many people to life with his health-giving, heavenly command, he revived three people brought back to life from infernal death; specifically, he revived the daughter of a ruler of the synagogue in his home, he commanded the only son of a widow to arise at the entrance of a gate, and he called Lazarus from his tomb.

3. His suffering, resurrection, and ascension.

The Jews therefore raged with anger, and encircling this just man with false accusations they delivered him to death and condemned him to be nailed to the cross. God the Father revived him from the dead on the third day after dissolving the afflictions of death, since it was impossible, as the apostle Peter says [Acts 2:24], for him to be bound among the inhabitants of the infernal regions. Then, [after] promising [to send] a Paraclete and instructing the apostles in heavenly doctrines, Jesus ascended as a victor to the heavens, promising anew with the angels as his witnesses that he would return to judge, as the history of the acts of the apostles relates: "This Jesus who was taken back from you will return in the same way as you saw him going into heaven" [Acts 1:11].

4. The apostles and the blessed Mary.

Then, after the wonderful glory of the Lord's ascension, which inspired the minds of believers to contemplate heavenly affairs by bruising the head of diabolical evilness, the holy apostles of our Lord and Saviour gathered with the blessed Mary, his mother, in one house

---

[3] This miracle had special significance for Gregory as bishop of Tours, because in the church of St Martin at Tours a mural on the north wall depicted Jesus Christ walking on the water: see L.Pietri (1983) 807, for the text of the inscription describing the mural, and Van Dam (1985) 242-3.

and always shared everything in common. No one said that something
was his own, but each always possessed everything in charity, as the
holy pen of the acts of the apostles narrates [Acts 4:34]. Then they
were sent throughout different regions to preach the word of God.

Although the blessed Mary had already been called [to live apart]
from this world, finally the passage of her life was completed, and all
the apostles gathered from their particular regions at her house. When
they heard that she must be taken from the world, they all kept watch
with her. And behold, the Lord Jesus came with his angels, and after
taking her soul he gave it to the angel Michael and left. At dawn the
apostles lifted her body on a bed, placed it in a tomb, and kept guard
over it, in anticipation of the arrival of the Lord. And behold, again the
Lord approached them. He took the holy body in a cloud and ordered it
to be brought to Paradise, where, after regaining her soul, Mary now
rejoices with his elect and enjoys the goodness of eternity that will
never perish.[4]

5. His cross and his miracles at Poitiers.

The cross of the Lord that was found by the empress Helena at
Jerusalem is venerated on Wednesday and Friday. Queen Radegund,
who is comparable to Helena in both merit and faith, requested relics of
this cross and piously placed them in a convent at Poitiers that she
founded out of her own zeal. She repeatedly sent servants to Jerusalem
and throughout the entire region of the East. These servants visited the
tombs of holy martyrs and confessors and brought back relics of them
all. After placing them in the silver reliquary with the holy cross itself,
she thereafter deserved to see many miracles.[5]

---

[4] This story represents apparently the first formulation of the doctrine of the
bodily Assumption of the Virgin in western orthodox theology: see van Esbroek
(1981). Although Krusch (1885) 489 n.6, suggests that Gregory had used a
written source, it is more likely that he learned of this doctrine from someone
who had visited the East: see Cameron (1978) 90, 93-4. Elsewhere Gregory
recorded how the archangel Michael and St Mary had received St Martin into
Paradise upon his death [*VM* 1.5].

[5] Early traditions had already associated the discovery of the True Cross
with the emperor Constantine, who reigned until 337, although his mother
Helena was not given credit for finding it until the end of the fourth century [*HF*
I.36]: see Hunt (1982) 28-49, and Drake (1985). Gregory was furthermore not

Of these miracles I will first mention this one that the Lord deigned to reveal during the days of his suffering. On the [Good] Friday before holy Easter when [the nuns] were spending the night in vigils without any light, about the third hour of the night a small light appeared before the altar in the shape of a spark. Then it was enlarged and scattered bright beams here and there. Slowly it began to rise higher, and after becoming a huge beacon it offered light for the dark night and for the congregation that was keeping vigil and praying. As the sky began to brighten it gradually faded until, upon the return of daylight to the lands, it vanished from the sight of the onlookers.

Often I heard how even the lamps that were lit in front of these relics bubbled up because of the divine power and dripped so much oil that frequently they filled a vessel underneath. But because of the foolishness of my closed mind I was never motivated to believe these stories until that power which is at present being revealed reproved my slow-witted hesitation.

For that reason I will describe what I saw with my own eyes. While visiting the tomb of St Hilary [at Poitiers], I happened out of respect to arrange a conversation with this queen [Radegund]. I entered the convent, greeted the queen, and bowed before the venerable cross and the holy relics of the saints. Then, at the conclusion of my prayer, I stood up. To my right was a burning lamp that I saw was overflowing with frequent drips. I call God as my witness, I thought that its con-

---

well-informed about the liturgical adoration of the True Cross at Jerusalem: see Frolow (1961) 162.

Radegund, the daughter of the king of Thuringia, had been captured by king Chlothar in c.531, who then married her. But after he had her brother killed, she left him, became a nun, and founded a convent in Poitiers [*HF* III.7, IX.39-42], whose most notable patron saint was its fourth-century bishop Hilary [*GC* 2]. For her convent she designated Agnes as abbess and adopted the monastic Rule composed by bishop Caesarius of Arles, who had died in 542 [*HF* IX.42]: see McCarthy (1960), Wemple (1981) 38-9, 149-58, 183-5, and Hochstetler (1987). Probably in 568 Radegund sent envoys to the Byzantine court at Constantinople, and probably in the next year she received relics of the True Cross from the emperor Justin II: see Cameron (1976), for the date and a discussion of the political and religious implications of the use of these relics as gifts of diplomacy; and Baudonivia, *Vita Radegundis* 16, ed. B.Krusch, *MGH*, SRM 2 (1888) 387-9, for the arrival of the relics at Poitiers. Radegund died in 587 [cf. *HF* IX.2, *GC* 104].

tainer was broken, because placed beneath it was a vessel into which the
overflowing oil dripped. I turned to the abbess [Agnes] and said: "Is
your thinking so irresponsible that you cannot provide an unbroken
lamp in which the oil can be burned, but instead you use a cracked lamp
from which the oil drips?" She replied: "My lord, such is not the case;
it is the power of the holy cross you are watching." Then I reconsidered
and remembered what I had heard earlier. I turned back to the lamp [that
was now] heaving in great waves like a boiling pot, overflowing in
swelling surges throughout that hour, and (I believe in order to censure
my incredulity) being more and more replenished, so that in the space
of one hour the container produced more than four times the oil that it
held.[6] Stunned, I was silent, and finally I proclaimed the power of the
venerable cross.

A girl named Chrodigildis was punished by the loss of her eyesight
while she was living in the territory of Le Mans after the death of her
father. Later, however, while the blessed queen Radegund was still
alive, at the command of king Chilperic she entered the rule of the
aforementioned convent. With the most blessed Radegund as a guide,
she bowed before the holy reliquary and there kept vigils with the other
nuns. When morning came and the others left, she remained in the
same place prostrate on the ground. In a vision it seemed to her as if
someone had opened her eyes. One eye was restored to health; while
she was still concerned about the other, suddenly she was awakened by
the sound of a door being unlocked and regained the sight of one eye.
There is no doubt that this was accomplished by the power of the cross.
The possessed, the lame, and also other ill people are often cured at this
place. Enough on this topic.

The nails of the Lord's cross, which held the blessed limbs, are
splendid and superior to all metal. They were found by the empress
Helena after the discovery of the holy cross itself. With two nails she
reinforced the bridle of the emperor so that whenever hostile peoples
resisted the emperor, they might more easily be dispersed by this
power. It is not unknown that the prophet Zachariah offered a predic-

---

[6] More literally, the container of the lamp that did not hold a *quartarius* of
oil now produced more than a *sextarius*, the equivalent of a little more than a
pint: see Weidemann (1982) II:343.

tion about these events; he says: "What is placed in the mouth of a horse will be holy to the Lord" [Zachariah 14:20].

At that time huge waves disturbed the Adriatic Sea, on which so many ships were wrecked and so many men were drowned that it was called the whirlpool of sailors. The far-sighted empress [Helena], concerned over the disasters of these miserable men, ordered one of the four nails to be thrown into the sea. She relied upon the pity of the Lord that he was able easily to calm the savage rolling of the waves. Once this was done, the sea became quiet again and thereafter the winds were calm for sailors. From then until today once sailors have piously set sail on the sanctified sea they have time for fasting, praying, and reciting psalms.[7]

Here is a rationale to account for the Lord's four nails. Two were driven in his palms and two in his feet. The question arises, why were there nails in his feet, which seem to hang from rather than stand on the holy cross? But a hole was clearly drilled in the upright post, and into this hole the end of a small board was inserted. The holy feet were nailed on top of this board as if they were the feet of a standing man.

The question arises, what was done with these nails? Two, as I said earlier, were inserted in a bridle, a third was thrown into the sea. Some claim that the fourth was affixed to [the diadem or helmet on] the head of a statue of Constantine which, so they say, is supposed to rise above the entire city [of Constantinople], with the result that what one might call a helmet of salvation crowns the entire fortification over which it towers.[8] Some claim that this bridle has great power, which can by no means be disputed. The emperor Justin experienced this power and publicly revealed it to his subjects. On account of some money Justin was tricked by a magician. When the ghost of a demon had been sent against him, for two nights he endured unbearable

---

[7] Gregory typically used the turbulent sea as a symbol of dangers and misfortunes in life: see de Nie (1985) 101-11.

[8] Other traditions accounted for the nails used in the crucifixion differently: see Frolow (1961) 167-9. This statue of Constantine on a column in Constantinople came to symbolize the invincibility of the city itself. Note that the association between these relics and Constantine also neatly represented a fundamental confusion in Byzantine political philosophy between Jesus Christ and the emperor, who both acted as mediators with God: see Dagron (1974) 37-9, 405-9.

threats;[9] but when on the third night he placed the bridle on his head, the enemy no longer had the means of threatening him. Once the instigator of this deceit was found, Justin executed him with a sword.

The nature of the power of this wood became apparent to me in this way. A man arrived who showed me a small robe that was made entirely of silk and that was very old. He claimed that the Lord's cross had been wrapped in this robe at Jerusalem. Because of my ignorance[10] this claim seemed outrageous, and I immediately asked how he had received such favor there that he was worthy [to acquire] these relics. For I knew not only that no one was ever judged worthy when this sacred wood was adored, but also that whoever approached improperly was kept away with whips. In reply he said: "As I was leaving Jerusalem, I met the abbot Futes, who had great favor with the empress Sophia [wife of Justin II]; for they had entrusted the entire East to this man as if it were his prefecture. I attached myself to this man, and when I was returning from the East I received from him both these relics of saints and this robe in which the holy cross was then always wrapped." After this man told me this story and gave me this robe, I confess, I dared to wash the robe and allow people with fevers to drink [the water]. But soon, as the divine power brought aid, they were healed. Then I even cut off some pieces and gave them to monks as a blessing. I gave one piece to an abbot who returned two years later and claimed under oath that it had healed twelve possessed people, three blind people, and two paralytics. He had placed [his piece of] the robe in the mouth of a mute man, and as soon as it touched his teeth and tongue, it restored his voice and speech. The promise of the Lord convinces us trustfully to believe this story; for the Lord said: "Believe

[9] The manuscript readings in Krusch (1920) 727, are preferable here: "...propter pecuniam emissamque sibi daemonis umbram intolerabiles...sustenuit insidias."

[10] *Rusticitas* was a word that Gregory used in many senses to denote the opposite of what was true, proper, civilized, and Christian; its range of meanings included "ignorance", "immorality", "uncouthness", and "paganism", and it could be used in either a neutral or a negative sense: see the introduction to Van Dam (forthcoming).

that you will receive everything which you have asked in my name and they will come to you" [Mark 11:24].[11]

6. The lance and other items from the Lord's suffering, and the tomb.

With regard to the lance, the reed, the sponge, the crown of thorns, and the column on which the Lord and Redeemer was whipped at Jerusalem: many who are filled with faith approach this column and tie around it cords they have woven; they receive these cords back as a blessing that will help against various illnesses.

They say that the thorns of the crown appear as if alive. But if its leaves seem to have withered, every day they become green again because of divine power.

Marvelous power appears from the tomb where the Lord's body lay. Often the ground is covered with a natural radiant brightness; then it is sprinkled with water and dug up, and from it tiny [clay] tokens are shaped and sent to different parts of the world. Often ill people acquire cures by means of these tokens. The fact that these tokens frequently deflect the approach of snakes is remarkable. But what do I rashly dare to say about them, since faith believes that everything that the sacred body touched is holy?[12]

7. The tunic of the Lord's body.

With regard to the holy body's tunic that was not sewn together but woven from top to bottom, the faith of the evangelist explains that it

[11] Justin II was emperor at Constantinople from 565 until 578. The identity of abbot Futes (or Photius) is uncertain: see Krusch (1885) 492 n.1, 883.

[12] Krusch (1885) 458, suggested that for some of his information about the Holy Land, here and elsewhere, Gregory had read a survey entitled *De situ terrae sanctae* that an archdeacon named Theodosius had composed between 518 and c.530: ed. P.Geyer, *CSEL* 39 (1898) 136-50 = *CChrL* 175 (1965) 115-25 = *PL* Suppl.4.1456-63, and trans. Wilkinson (1977) 63-71. Gregory and Theodosius may also simply have used similar sources: see Wilkinson o.c. 66, 184-92. Another mural in the church of St Martin at Tours depicted this column on which Jesus had been whipped, as well as the church at Jerusalem and the throne of the apostle James [*GM* 26]: see L.Pietri (1983) 807, for the text of the inscription describing the mural, and Van Dam (1985) 243. The distribution of clay tokens as "blessings" for pilgrims was common at holy sites in the East: see Vikan (1984).

would be disposed of by lot in accordance with the prophecy [in a psalm] of David. For he says: "They divided my garments among themselves and they cast lots for my clothing" [John 19:24, quoting Psalm 22:18]. But I cannot be silent about what I have heard from some people about this tunic of the immaculate lamb. They say that it is still in the city of Galatea, in a church named for the holy archangels. This city is about one hundred and fifty miles from Constantinople. In the church is a very obscure crypt where this garment was stored in a wooden box. Pious believers most assiduously adored this box that was justly deserving [of adoration because] it held this garment [that] was worthy both to touch and to clothe the body of the Lord.[13]

8. The miracles of the church of St Mary.

The glorious Mary, Mother of Christ, is believed to have been a virgin after the birth [of Christ] just as before the birth. As I already mentioned, she was translated among a chorus of singing angels to Paradise, where the Lord had already gone. Her church was constructed by the emperor Constantine and shone forth as an impressive building. Columns were brought to it, but they could not be raised because of their size; the circumference of each was sixteen feet. Each day the workmen were worn out by their futile efforts, [until] the holy Virgin appeared to the architect in a vision and said: "Do not despair. For I will show you how these columns can be raised." Then she showed him what scaffolding was appropriate, how the pulleys were hung, and for what task the ropes were stretched. She added: "Have with you three boys from the schools, [so that] you can complete the task with their assistance." After the architect awoke and prepared what had been commanded, he summoned three boys from the schools and very quickly set up the columns. People had the opportunity to witness a wonderful miracle, because three boys, without the benefit of previous experience, raised what many strong men could not raise. The holy festival of Mary is celebrated in the middle of the eleventh month [January].[14]

---

[13] Galatea is probably the city of Galatz, north of Constantinople/Istanbul in Romania: see Vieillard-Troiekouroff (1976) 431.

[14] Gregory presumably alluded here to the martyrium in honor of the Virgin in the Valley of Jehoshaphat outside Jerusalem: see Krautheimer (1965) 51, and

Relics of Mary are kept in the oratory of an estate at Marsat, in the
territory of Clermont. When the day of her festival was near, I travelled
to the oratory to keep vigils. As I was hurrying to the oratory in the
dark night, I noted at a distance such a bright light shining through its
windows that I thought many torches and candles were burning inside.
I supposed that some of the pious had preceded me to keep vigils. I
approached the door, knocked, but found no one. After discovering that
the door was locked tight with a key, I realized that everything was
happening in silence. Why say more? I sent for the custodian whose
task was to look after the place [and requested] that he of course bring a
key and unlock the door. While he was coming, I lit a candle outside.
Meanwhile the door swung open on its own, and I entered. But in the
glow of my candle the bright light that I had admired from the outside
disappeared—I think because of the blackness of my sins. Inside I
could find nothing from which that bright light had originated except
the power of the glorious Virgin.[15]

9. The boy [who was] thrown into a fire.

I will not pass over events in the East that support the catholic
faith.[16] The son of a Jewish glass-worker was studying and learning the

---

Vieillard-Troiekouroff (1976) 432. Gregory used several systems of chronology,
among them one in which March was considered the first month of the year: see
des Graviers (1946).

[15] At least by the ninth century this estate belonged to the church of St
Martin at Tours: see Vieillard-Troiekouroff (1976) 158. Because Gregory felt
himself to be specially associated with St Martin, perhaps his visit indicates that
the church of St Martin already in the sixth century owned this property: see
Weidemann (1982) I:206, 233, II:109, who also argues that Gregory visited
Marsat after he became a priest but before he became bishop of Tours in 573.
Another possibility is that the estate belonged to Gregory's family, who in fact
owned other lands in the Limagne [GM 83]: see Wood (1983) 40-1. Eventually
Gregory carried with him a gold cross containing relics of St Mary and St
Martin [GM 10].

[16] Evagrius, a lawyer at Antioch who was an almost exact contemporary of
Gregory, included a similar story in his history of eastern Christianity during the
fifth and sixth centuries and placed it at Constantinople during the episcopacy of
Menas from 536 to 552: see Evagrius, *Historia ecclesiastica* IV.36, ed. J.Bidez
and L.Parmentier (1898) 185-6. Despite canonical restrictions, Jews did
occasionally attend mass: see Blumenkranz (1960) 84-8.

alphabet with Christian boys. One day while the ritual of mass was being celebrated in the church of the blessed Mary, this Jewish boy approached with the other young boys to partake of the glorious body and blood of the Lord. After receiving the holy [eucharist], he happily returned to his father's house. His father was working, and between embraces and kisses the boy mentioned what he had so happily received. Then his father, an enemy of Christ the Lord and his laws, said: "If you have communicated with these boys and forgotten your ancestral worship, then to avenge this insult to the law of Moses I will step forward against you as a merciless murderer." And he seized the boy and threw him into the mouth of a raging furnace; he was persistent and added wood so the furnace would burn hotter. But that compassion that had once sprinkled the dew of a cloud on the three Hebrew boys who had been thrown into a Chaldaean furnace [cf. Daniel 3:8-30] was not lacking. For it did not allow this boy, even though lying on a pile of coals in the middle of the fire, to be consumed in the least. When his mother heard that the father had evidently decided to incinerate their son, she hurried to save him. But when she saw the fire leaping from the open mouth of the furnace and flames raging here and there, she threw her barrette to the ground. Her hair was disheveled; she wailed that she was in misery and filled the city with her cries. When the Christians learned what had been done, they all rushed to such an evil sight; after the flames had been beaten back from the mouth of the furnace, they found the boy reclining as if on very soft feathers. When they pulled him out, they were all astonished that he was unhurt. The place was filled with shouts, and so everyone blessed God. Then they shouted that they should throw the instigator of this crime into these flames. Once he was thrown in, the fire burned him so completely that somehow scarcely a tiny piece of his bones was left. When the Christians asked the young boy what sort of shield he had had in the flames, he said: "The woman who was sitting on the throne in that church where I received the bread from the table and who was cradling a young boy in her lap covered me with her cloak, so that the fire did not devour me." There is hence no doubt that the blessed Mary had appeared to him. Then, having acknowledged the catholic faith, the young boy believed in the name of the Father and the Son and the Holy Spirit. After he and his mother had been baptized in the waters of salvation, they were reborn. In that city many Jews were saved by this example.[17]

At Jerusalem there is a truly great monastery that has many members. Often the devotion of the people presents many gifts at that spot; indeed, the greatest gifts are bestowed by order of the emperor. At some time it happened that the supplies necessary for living were lacking because of impoverishment. When they did not receive food at their meals for one day, and then for another, an outspoken group of monks complained to the abbot and said: "Give us food, or else allow us to go somewhere else where it is possible to support ourselves; otherwise, we are leaving without your permission so that we do not die of starvation." After they spoke, the abbot replied: "Most beloved brothers, let us pray, and the Lord will provide us with food. For it cannot happen that there is insufficient wheat in a monastery dedicated to her [Mary] who offered from her womb the fruit of life to a starving world." After they kept vigils and chanted psalms for the entire night, at daybreak they found all the buildings of their granary so stuffed with wheat that it was hardly possible for the door to be opened. Having then received food, they gave thanks to God.

Many years later food was again lacking. The monks complained to the abbot, who said: "Let us keep vigils and pray to the Lord, and perhaps he will deign to send sustenance." Then they knelt on the pavement of the church. During the night they kept a vigil by singing psalms, hymns, and religious verses. After matins when they fell asleep, an angel of the Lord came and placed on the altar an immense pile of gold. The doors of the building had been bolted. When the abbot and the monks awoke at dawn to celebrate the liturgical office, they saw the heap of gold on the altar. The abbot said to the custodian of the church: "Which of the prefects entered here and brought these

---

[17] Although Gregory may have believed that Jews had been responsible for the crucifixion of Jesus Christ [*GM* 3], his rather nonchalant attitude toward the murder of this boy's father is still remarkable [cf. *GM* 21]. Usually in sixth-century Gaul Jews enjoyed toleration, although occasionally Christians harassed them [cf.*HF* VI.5, 17, VIII.1]: see Bachrach (1977) 44-65, and Wallace-Hadrill (1983) 390-403. Most notably, in 576 bishop Avitus of Clermont sanctioned the destruction of the synagogue on Easter and than gave the Jews in the city the choice of converting or leaving [*HF* V.11]: see Brennan (1985a), and Goffart (1985).

objects?" He replied: "After your departure no one had access here, but I kept it bolted tight and had the key to the door with me until you arose to sound the bell." Then the abbot along with his monks was astounded and realized [this was] a gift from heaven. He gave thanks to God, gathered the gold, collected the supplies necessary for living, and generously assisted the men entrusted [to him]. But it is not surprising that the blessed Virgin, who conceived without intercourse with a man and who remained a virgin even after the birth [of Christ], effortlessly supplied her monks.

10. The fire [controlled] by the power of the relics of St Mary.

Once I was as usual wearing relics of this blessed Virgin along with those of the holy apostles and of the blessed Martin that had been placed in a gold cross. As I was travelling along the road, I noticed, not far from the road, that a poor man's cottage was on fire. The cottage had been covered with leaves that served as ready kindling for the flames. With his children and wife the poor man was running about carrying water, but the flames were not dying down. Lifting the cross from my chest I held it up against the fire; soon, in the presence of the holy relics the entire fire stopped so [suddenly], as if there had been no blaze.

11. John the Baptist and his relics at Bazas.

John the Baptist was in fact kept in prison because [king] Herod was tricked by Herodias, his brother's wife [Matthew 14:3; Mark 6:17]. At that time a woman had departed from Gaul for Jerusalem in the hope that she might deserve [to enjoy] the presence of our Lord and Saviour. But she heard that the blessed John was to be beheaded. Quickly she went there, and with bribes she begged the executioner that he not deny her permission to collect the dripping blood. As the executioner struck, the woman held ready a silver vessel and piously collected some blood after the head of the martyr had been cut off. After carefully storing the blood in a flask, she brought it to her homeland. Once a cathedral had been constructed in his honor at Bazas, she placed the flask in the holy altar.

12. The gem formed by divine power at Bazas.

Since I have mentioned Bazas, I think it worthwhile to relate a miracle that the Lord bestowed on that city. At a time when the city was surrounded by Huns during a long siege, the bishop who then presided walked about chanting psalms and praying for an entire night and requested, not the aid of any man, but only the pity of the Lord. He continually urged everyone to pray and not to cease, claiming that the requests of the humble would enter the gates of heaven. The enemy meanwhile was plundering villas in the neighborhood, burning homes, and destroying fields and vineyards by letting the livestock loose. But divine power was quick to assist a bishop who was persisting in a good cause. One night it appeared to the king of the barbarians as if men dressed in white, who were chanting psalms and [carrying] burning candles, were encircling the walls of the city. In his anger the king said: "What sort of boldness and false security is this, that these people under siege can shout unfamiliar chants and praises, as if we were of no concern? Indeed, these people deserve to be destroyed." Immediately he sent envoys to the city who asked what these things signified. But the people in the city replied that they did not know what the messengers were talking about and that they had witnessed none of these things. On another night the king saw what appeared to be a great ball of fire descend over the city. He said: "If these besieged people mock us and do not fear us, at least the wrath of heaven is consuming them." But when he did not observe any fire breaking out in the city, he sent again and asked what it was that he had seen. Again the people denied that they had seen anything at all. Then king Gauseric said: "If they do not know about these things, it is obvious that their God is helping them." Immediately he left that region.

Then the bishop called together the citizens, kept vigils, and cele-brated the ritual of mass [in gratitude] for the liberation of his congre-gation. As he did so, he looked up and noticed over the altar three drops falling apparently from the vault. These drops were similar to a crystal in size and clearness, but much brighter. In their amazement everyone was completely stunned and only stared. Since no one dared to touch the drops, a priest named Peter, who, as the very event demonstrated, possessed great merit, held out a silver paten and tried to catch the drops. While the drops were spinning in an indeterminate circle over the altar, they flowed unto the paten and immediately fused together, as if they formed one extremely beautiful gem. By an obvious deduction it was evident that this had taken place in opposition to the evil heresy of Arianism, which was hateful to God and which was spreading at that time. It was furthermore acknowledged that the holy Trinity was bound

in a single equality of power and could not be pulled apart by chattering
[arguments]. The congregation rejoiced in knowing that this gift had
been granted them by God. The people collected gold and precious
jewels and made a cross in which they deposited this gem. In the presence of this gem all the other jewels immediately fell out. The bishop
then realized that heavenly things could not associate with earthly
things. A cross was made from pure gold. The bishop set the gem in
the middle of the intersection [of the arms of the cross] and offered it for
the congregation to adore. Immediately the enemy fled, as we mentioned, and the city was freed. Since then many ill people who drink
the wine or the water in which the gem has been washed are quickly
restored to health. Whenever the gem is adored, it appears clear if the
man is free from sin; but if, as usually happens, a man has brought
some guilt upon his human weakness, to him the gem appears totally
opaque. The gem wonderfully distinguishes between innocent and
guilty, since it is black for one but clear for another.[18]

13. The relics of St John brought to Saint-Jean-de-Maurienne.
    A woman set out from Saint-Jean-de-Maurienne and sought relics
of the forerunner [John the Baptist]. She pledged herself by the bond of
an oath that she would not leave that place until she was worthy to
receive a relic from his limbs. When the inhabitants of the region said
this was impossible, every day she kneeled before the tomb and prayed
that some relic from his holy limbs be given her, as I have said. In
this pursuit she spent an entire year, and then likewise another year,
always praying, always making her request. As the third year
approached and she felt that her prayer was not having any effect, she
threw herself before the tomb and insisted that she would not stand up
again until her petition was received by the saint. On the seventh day,

---

[18] Not only does this bishop remain unidentified, but there is also
uncertainty over the identity of the barbarians who besieged Bazas. Krusch
(1885) 496 n.1 and (1920) 728, and Rouche (1979) 19, suggest that these
barbarians were Vandals and that Gregory was referring to Geiseric, king of the
Vandals from c.428 until 477; the problem with this identification is that the
Vandals had already left Gaul for Spain in 409: see Courtois (1955) 38-51.
Courcelle (1964) 93-5, 289 n.2, refers instead to the siege of Bazas by the
Visigoths and Alans in 414; Vieillard-Troiekouroff (1976) 50, suggests an attack
on Bazas by Visigoths in the later fifth century.

when she was becoming weak from fasting, there appeared over the altar a gleaming thumb, wonderfully bright and clear. The woman recognized this gift from God and rose from the pavement. She acquired a small gold reliquary and put in it [the thumb] that the Lord had given and that she had deserved. So she happily returned to her own [city]. What the Lord said in the Gospel was fulfilled in this woman: "Amen, I say to you that if a man will have persevered in his knocking, and if another man does not get up because he is a friend, yet he rises because of his boldness and gives him whatever he needs" [Luke 11:8].[19]

Later three bishops arrived from their own cities to worship in this place and wished to take a piece from this relic. It was placed in the open, but in no way could they remove anything. Then, while keeping vigils one night they prayed that they might be worthy of some relic from the thumb. They placed a linen cloth beneath the thumb, and while they tried to remove a piece, a single drop of blood fell from the thumb unto the linen cloth. Once they saw this, they kept vigils two more nights. Then, while they knelt before the holy altar and asked that they be worthy of something greater from the thumb, two more drops fell from it. In their happiness they piously collected what the Lord had given and divided the linen cloth with its drops according to the number of the Lord's servants. With great respect the three bishops brought these relics to their own cities.

Because the site of Saint-Jean-de-Maurienne extended to the [border of the] city of Turin, at the time when Rufus was bishop his archdeacon said to him: "It is not proper that this relic be kept in that insignificant place. Rise, take it, and bring it to the cathedral at Turin which is considered more reputable. The bishop replied to him that he did not dare to do this. The archdeacon said: "I will fetch this relic, if you agree." The bishop said: "Do whatever pleases you." Then the archdeacon went to the site, and while keeping vigils he put his hand on the reliquary. Soon he went mad, burned with a fever, and on the third day expired. A great fear arose in everyone, and no one dared to tamper again with the sacred relics.

---

[19] At least by the fourth century the tomb of John the Baptist was thought to be at Sebaste: see Wilkinson (1977) 169. A tenth-century charter named this woman as Tigris/Tygris: ed. B.Krusch, *MGH*, SRM 3 (1896) 533-4.

14. The relics of St John placed in a monastery of St Martin.

At Tours, while I was depositing relics of the forerunner [John the Baptist] in an oratory located in a courtyard of [the church of] St Martin, a blind man dropped his cane and received his sight. A possessed man called upon the power of the blessed John and bishop Martin and was cleansed after the demon was expelled. One of the girls responsible for filling a lamp with oil entered the oratory, carrying a candle to do her job. After filling and lighting the lamp, she tied a rope to it, hoisted [the lamp] up in the air, fastened [the rope] with a knot looped around a nail in the wall, and left. As she was leaving, the candle in her hand went out. She quickly returned to the lamp, but she did not reach to light the candle or to untie the knot in the rope. While she was uncertain and thought about the dilemma, suddenly a spark fell from the lamp and lit the candle in her hand. So, with the help of the light that preceded her, she went where she wished.

Some say that in this oratory oil bubbles over from the lamp. For relics of the holy cross are also kept there.[20]

15. The relics of St John in the village of Langeais.

Within the territory of Tours, at the village of Langeais, a woman who lived there made up dough on the Lord's Day and formed a loaf of bread. After separating her coals she covered the loaf with glowing cinders for baking. As she did this, immediately her right hand was scorched by divine fire and began to burn. Screaming and weeping, she went to the church of this village in which relics of the blessed John [the Baptist] were kept. She prayed at length and vowed that on this day consecrated by the divine name she would never again work, but would devote it only to prayer. On the following night she made a candle as tall as herself. Then she spent the night in prayer, and during the entire night she held the candle in her own hand. The burning pains were quenched, and she left with her health.[21]

---

[20] Vieillard-Troiekouroff (1976) 309, suggests that this oratory should perhaps be identified with the baptistery in which Gregory mentioned [*HF* X.31] that he had placed relics of St John and St Sergius [*GM* 96]; L.Pietri (1983) 399-402, disagrees.

[21] Gregory claimed that bishop Martin of Tours had founded this church at Langeais [*HF* X.31]: see Vieillard-Troiekouroff (1976) 127-8, and L.Pietri (1983)

16. The Jordan river.

Since I have mentioned John the Baptist, it is appropriate that I say something about the Jordan river. Two streams flow from Mt. Paneas [Mt. Hermon], one named Jor, the other Dan. They flow on each side of the city of Paneas, which was previously known as Caesarea Philippi; below this city their streams as well as their names are joined, and they become the Jordan which flows all the way to the city of Jericho and beyond. In it is the spot where the Lord was baptized. In fact, at one bend the water in which lepers are now cleansed swirls around. For when the lepers have arrived, they are bathed frequently in the water until they are cleansed of their illness. While they wait there, they are kept at public expense; once healed, they return to their own homes. When it enters the Dead Sea, five miles from that spot, the Jordan river loses its name. For this sea is called dead because it was whirled about by the destruction of Sodom and the other cities, and its water was mixed with asphalt. Hence some call it the Sea of Asphalt. Someone who does not know how to swim floats on top of its water, and sulphur collects around its banks.

17. The springs at Levida [Beth-Harâm].

At the city of Levida there are hot springs in which Joshua the son of Nun used to bathe. There lepers are likewise cleansed. This city is twelve miles from Jericho. Near Jericho there are trees which produce wool. On these trees grow fruits similar to gourds that have tough shells around them but inside are full of wool. Some say that clothing used to be made from this wool for Joshua the son of Nun. But still today [these trees] produce such fine wool; I have seen some that people gathered, and I marveled at its whiteness and fineness.

---

58 n.171. Although contemporary councils prohibited people from working and various other activities on Sundays and festival days in honor of saints, Gregory's miracle stories provide many examples of people who became ill or suffered disaster because they had "insulted" these days [*HF* X.30]: see Wood (1979) 62-5, and Van Dam (1985) 285-8.

18. The relics of the blessed Mary.

Previously I saw a man named Johannes who had departed from Gaul as a leper. He said that he had waited for an entire year at that spot where I said the Lord had been baptized. Frequently he washed himself in the river; when his skin was transformed for the better, he was cured and restored to his earlier health. From Jerusalem he received relics of the blessed Mary. He set out for his fatherland but decided first to visit Rome. As soon as he entered the vast mountains of Italy, he met bandits. Immediately he was robbed of his clothing; even the reliquary in which he carried the blessed relics was seized. For these highwaymen thought that gold coins were in the reliquary, and after breaking the lock they closely examined everything. When they found no money in it, they took out the relics and threw them in a fire. After beating the man, they left. Although half unconscious, the man got up to collect the ashes of the relics that had burned. He found the relics lying unburned on top of smoldering embers. He was astonished that the linen cloth in which the relics were wrapped was so spotless that one might think it had been not tossed on coals but soaked in water. Happily he gathered everything up and set out on the road he was travelling; he reached Gaul in safety.[22] I have seen many people who bathed either in the Jordan river or in the springs of the city of Levida and were healed of this disease.

19. The church at Tours [containing] relics of St Mary and John the Baptist.

At Tours there is a church dedicated in the names of the Virgin St Mary and John the Baptist; in it divine vengeance has appeared to perjurers. Once a man entered this church to commit perjury. He stood before the altar, and when he raised his hand to swear a false oath, immediately he fell over backwards. He struck his head on the pavement so hard that he was hardly conscious when he could be helped up. Once he had revived, he publicly confessed the deception of perjury that he had concealed. I myself saw men from Tours commit perjury in that

---

[22] This Johannes may well be the deacon Johannes [*GM* 87] and "our deacon" [*GM* 1] who told Gregory other stories about the Holy Land: see Krusch (1885) 458-9.

spot. They were condemned by divine judgement so severely that within a year they had expired from the world.[23]

20. The miracles of the statue at Paneas.

The city of Paneas is located, as I said, at the source of the Jordan river. In the city there is a statue made from completely pure electrum, on which the likeness of our Redeemer is said to be displayed. As I have heard from many people who have seen it, there is a marvelous brightness in its face. Lest this seem absurd to anyone, it is proper to quote what Eusebius of Caesarea wrote about this statue. He says: "It is a fact that the woman who according to the Gospels suffered from a discharge of blood and was healed by the Saviour was a citizen of this city. Even now her house in that city is on display. In front of the doors of her house is a pedestal, set up on a mound. Prominently exhibited on the pedestal is a bronze statue of the woman herself, as if kneeling and stretching her hands in supplication. Next to it is another statue, likewise cast from bronze, in the guise of a man elegantly wrapped in a robe and extending his right hand to the woman. At the foot of this statue, on its pedestal, a plant of a unique kind grows. When this plant has blossomed, it usually extends to the fringe of the bronze robe that clothes the statue. Once this growing plant has touched the robe with its top shoot, it absorbs powers from the robe that can drive away all diseases and illnesses. Hence, whatever bodily infirmity there might be vanishes after a sip of a drink made from this healing plant. But if the plant is cut down before it grows and touches the hem of the bronze fringe, it acquires no powers at all. Some say that this statue was cast with the likeness of the face of Jesus. The statue is still standing now, and I have seen it with my own eyes. It is not surprising if the pagans who believed would appear to offer a memorial of this sort on behalf of the blessings they had received from the Saviour; for even now we see icons and pictures of the apostles

---

[23] Krusch (1885) 451-2, suggests that Gregory may here be referring to the perjury of Pelagius, who had terrorized the citizens of Tours before dying of a fever in 586 [*HF* VIII.40]. Bishops Ommatius and Injuriosus had built this church dedicated to St Mary and John the Baptist during the first half of the sixth century, and bishop Eufronius had restored it after a fire in 558: see Vieillard-Troiekouroff (1976) 327, and L.Pietri (1983) 358-63.

Peter and Paul and of the Saviour himself being designed and painted."
Eusebius has recorded these facts.[24]

21. The Jew who stole an image of Christ.

For even now at this time Christ is cherished with such love
through a perfect faith that believers who remember his law in the
tablets of their heart also hang a painted image of him in churches and
houses to record his power in visible tablets. But in this too the eternal
enemy of the human race reveals himself to be envious. For after a Jew
had often looked at an image of this sort that had been painted on a
panel and attached to the wall of a church, he said: "Behold the seducer,
who has humbled me and my people!" So, coming in at night, he
stabbed the image with a dagger, pried it from the wall, concealed it
under his clothes, carried it home, and prepared to burn it in a fire. But
a marvelous event took place that without doubt was a result of the
power of God. For blood flowed from the wound where the image had
been stabbed. This wicked assassin was so obsessed with rage that he
did not notice the blood. But after he had made his way through the
darkness of a cloudy night to his house, he brought a light and realized
that he was completely covered with blood. Fearing lest his crime
become obvious, he hid the panel he had stolen in an obscure spot; nor
did he dare any more to touch what he had wickedly presumed to carry
away. At dawn the Christians came to the house of God. When they
did not find the icon, they were upset and asked what had happened.
Then they noticed the trail of blood. They followed it and came to the
house of the Jew. They asked about the panel but learned nothing
certain. But they searched carefully for the panel and found it in a
corner of a small room belonging to the Jew. They restored the panel
to the church; they crushed the thief beneath stones.

---

[24] The Greek historian Eusebius had written a "Chronicle" and an
"Ecclesiastical History" that both covered events into the early fourth century.
For information about the history of the early church Gregory found his works
very useful [*HF* 1 praef., II praef.]. But since he could not read Greek, Gregory
certainly used the Latin translations (and continuations) of the "Chronicle" by
Jerome (d.420), and of the "Ecclesiastical History" by Rufinus (d.410). In this
chapter Gregory quoted, almost verbatim, from Rufinus, *Historia ecclesiastica*
VII.18, ed. Th.Mommsen, in *Eusebius Werke, vol.2: Die Kirchengeschichte*, ed.
E.Schwartz = *GCS* 9.2 (1908) 673.

22. Another picture of the Lord Christ.

At Narbonne in the principal cathedral which rejoices [to have] relics of the martyr St Genesius[25] there is a picture which shows our Lord on the cross, girded as it were with a linen [loincloth]. This picture was constantly observed by the congregation. But a terrifying person appeared to the priest Basileus in a vision and said: "All of you are clothed in various garments, but you see me always naked. Come now, as quickly as possible cover me with a curtain!" But the priest did not understand the vision, and when day came he remembered nothing at all. Again the man appeared to him; but the priest did not think it important. Three days after the second vision the man [appeared again,] struck [the priest] with heavy blows, and said: "Did I not tell you to cover me with a curtain, so that I would not be seen naked? But none of this has been done by you. Come now," he said, "and cover with a linen cloth the picture in which I appear on the cross; otherwise a quick death might befall you." The priest was upset and very afraid, and mentioned the vision to his bishop, who immediately ordered a curtain to be hung over [the picture]. And the picture is now on display but covered in this way. Even if it is briefly exposed for viewing, soon it is concealed by the lowered curtain, lest it be seen uncovered.[26]

[25] The identity of this martyr Genesius is uncertain, not least because Gregory mentioned three martyrs named Genesius, only one of whom had perhaps existed [*GM* 66, 67-68, 73].

[26] The hostile reaction to this icon or painting emphasizes how for early Christians the representation of Christ on the cross had posed fundamental theological and artistic questions about the proper relationship between his divine and human natures. Theologians found it difficult to harmonize the demands of Christology and soteriology. Christology required the perfect and complete union of Christ's two natures, while insisting that his divine nature was impassible and immortal; soteriology required Christ to suffer and die on the cross. In the face of such fundamentally incompatible requirements artists variously depicted Christ on the cross as dead or alive, with closed or open eyes, slumped or erect, clothed or unclothed: see Kartsonis (1986) 28-39, 127.

This cathedral had been constructed in the early 440s by bishop Rusticius of Narbonne: see Marrou (1970), and Vieillard-Troiekouroff (1976) 185-8. But Gregory gave no date for this particular incident: see Wessel (1967), for some artistic criteria, and Rouche (1987) 453-7, for early medieval attitudes toward nudity. During the fifth and sixth centuries most of the theological

42   TRANSLATION

23. The springs in Spain.
This well-known miracle happened at the Spanish springs that the province of Lusitania offers. In the plain of Osset there is a pool that was built long ago, skillfully sculpted from different types of marble in the shape of a cross. Over it a glistening, very tall shrine was constructed by the Christians. When the holy day following the cycle of the departing year was then approaching, the day on which the Lord confounded his betrayer and offered the mystical supper to his disciples, the citizens and their bishop met at that place. Already they sniffed the fragrance of a sacred aroma. Then the bishop offered a prayer, and they ordered the doors of the shrine to be sealed shut and awaited the arrival of the Lord's power. Three days later on the sabbath [Easter Saturday] people gathered for baptism. The bishop came with the citizens and after inspecting the seals opened the doors that had been closed. [What had happened] is extraordinary to report! The pool they had left empty they now found full. The pool was packed with a high mass of water, just as wheat is usually piled over the mouths of bushel baskets. You could see waves rippling here and there which did not spill over the other side. Once the water had been sanctified by exorcism and oil had been sprinkled over it, all the people drank as a sign of devotion. Then, for their own salvation they each carried back home a container full of water, intending to protect their fields and vineyards by sprinkling the beneficial water. And although many jars were filled with no limit imposed, the mass of water never decreased. But once the first child was immersed, soon the water receded; after everyone had been baptized,

---

controversies over Christology took place in the eastern empire: see Pelikan (1971) 226-77 and (1974) 37-61, and Baus, Beck, Ewig and Vogt (1980) 93-121, 421-63. Gregory himself exemplifies how little most Gallic churchmen knew about eastern theology and about Byzantine affairs in general. But the one region still in contact with the eastern Mediterranean, either directly or by way of Byzantine Italy, was southeastern Gaul. Men in Narbonne might have heard about some of these eastern theological controversies: see Markus (1978), for the possible influence of Byzantine notions about the cult of icons. Is it significant that the priest who was initially warned by the dreams had a Greek name?

the waters reversed, and as they appeared from an unknown source, so they disappeared by an unknown drain.[27]

24. People who did not honor this place.

There was a heretic who did not fear God, did not venerate this holy place, and did not believe in his heart. I will not pass over in silence the miracle that God deigned to demonstrate through him in order to strengthen his believers' faith. The man arrived with a herd of horses. Once the packs had been unloaded, he ordered that stalls be prepared for the horses in the church and that they be stabled there. The wretched man ignored what the local inhabitants told him about the place. Then, about midnight he was struck with a fever. Barely able to breathe, he repented (although later than he should have) and commanded the horses to be removed from the building. For in that region, although he was subordinate to the king, he still had great power. The horses were removed from the church. The man turned on himself and began to cut his body with his own teeth. Because of his fury his servants were unable immediately to restrain him. Finally he was subdued, but he died in the hands of his servants.

Once Theudigisel, king of this region, saw this miracle that had happened at the fountains that were sacred to God, he thought to himself and said: "It is a trick of the Romans"—by Romans they refer to men who accept our [catholic Nicene] Christianity—"that this happened, and it is not the power of God." The next year the king came and secured the door with his own seals in addition to the seal of the bishop. He also posted guards around the church, in order perhaps to apprehend the accomplice who plotted this subterfuge and whose ingenuity allowed the water to flow into the fountains. The next year he did the same. In the third year he gathered many men and ordered trenches to be dug around the church to prevent water from perhaps being channeled into the fountain by underground pipes. Their trenches were twenty-five feet deep and fifteen feet wide. But nothing could be found

---

[27] Osset was near Seville. Since the date of Easter was difficult to compute, Gregory preferred to correlate it with the filling of these springs at Osset and the equally miraculous filling of a baptismal pool at Embrun, also on the anniversary of the Lord's Supper [*HF* V.17, VI.43, *GC* 68]. For Gregory springs served as symbols of spiritual regeneration: see de Nie (1985) 93-101.

hidden [in the ground]. When facing imminent death (due, I think, to the arrogance of this search), he was unworthy the next year to see the day when this mystery is celebrated, because he had presumed to investigate the secret of divine power. In that place there are relics of St Stephen the deacon.[28]

25. The man who stole a knife at this place.

Because this fountain was filled by divine command for the celebration of baptism, as I already said, and because once it had been filled people were eager to drink from it, one man took a jug and extended it for filling by the priest who distributed this water. While the old [priest] was filling the jug, in the pressing crowd of people the man reached out to another's belt and stole his knife. After hiding this knife in his sheath, he reached out to take the jug that he had given the priest. He took the jug and moved away to another spot; but he was unable to discover a single drop of water in the jug. He was very perplexed. Once he realized that this had happened to him because he was a thief, he returned the knife he had stolen to its owner. After holding out his jug a second time, he received it back full of water.

The people there are heretics: they witness these great deeds but are not motivated to believe. They never cease skillfully to reject the sacraments of the divine teachings with the chattering of wrong interpretations. But the power of the Lord destroys and disorders his opposition.

26. The tomb of the apostle James.

The apostle James, who was also called the brother of the Lord, is said to have been ordained a bishop by our Lord Jesus Christ. After the glorious ascension of the Lord, James attempted to enlighten Jews who had wandered from the way of righteousness. He was thrown from the pinnacle of the temple and crushed when a fuller struck his head with a

---

[28] Theudigisel was briefly king of the Visigoths in Spain from 548 until 549 [*HF* III.30], although Gregory implied here that he reigned longer: see Thompson (1969) 16, and Collins (1983) 38. Visigoths often referred to catholic Nicene Christianity as the religion of the Romans [*GM* 78-79], and occasionally referred to their own Arianism as the "catholic faith": see Thompson (1969) 40.

club. He gave up his spirit and was buried on the Mount of Olives in a tomb that he had previously built for himself and in which he had buried Zacharias and Simeon. These [are the traditions] about the apostle James.[29]

27. The tomb and church of the apostle St Peter.

In order to demonstrate humility the apostle Peter ordered that his head be tonsured. He was ordained a bishop by the other apostles and founded his see at Rome. An oration by Peter and Paul exposed and refuted the cunning of Simon Magus. Still today at Rome there are two small indentations in the stone upon which the blessed apostles knelt and delivered their oration to the Lord against that Simon Magus. When rain water has collected in these indentations, ill people gather it; once they drink it, it soon restores their health.

As I already said, the apostle St Peter faced crucifixion after his wars against [the emperor] Nero and against Simon [Magus]. Since he had finished the struggle for the noble trophy, he requested that he be crucified with his feet upwards toward heaven; for he insisted that he was unworthy to be elevated [on the cross] in the same manner as the Lord. Then, after sending his living spirit to the stars, he was buried in the church that for a long time has been called the Vatican. This church has four rows of truly spectacular columns, ninety-six in all. There are four more columns at the altar, which make a total of one hundred, excepting those that support the ciborium over the tomb. The tomb is located beneath the altar and is quite inaccessible. Whoever wishes to pray comes to the top of the tomb after unlocking the railings that surround the spot; a small opening is exposed, and the person inserts his head in the opening and requests whatever is necessary. No delay will result if only a just prayer of petition is offered. But if someone wishes to take away a blessed relic, he weighs a little piece of cloth on

---

[29] Since Gregory believed that Mary had remained a virgin after the birth of Jesus Christ [*HF* I praef., *GM* 9, *VJ* 36], he elsewhere claimed that this James had been the son of Joseph and another wife and was therefore a half-brother of Jesus [*HF* I.22], and that he had been martyred with the evangelist Mark [*HF* I.26]. Zacharias (or Zechariah) was the father of John the Baptist, and was thought to have died as a martyr. Simeon was presumably the "righteous and devout man" who blessed the baby Jesus at Jerusalem with the *Nunc dimittis* [quoted in *GM* praef.]; so he was a "martyr" by his witness, not by his death.

a pair of scales and lowers it into [the tomb]; then he keeps vigils, fasts, and earnestly prays that the power of the apostle will assist his piety. [What happens next] is extraordinary to report! If the man's faith is strong, when the piece of cloth is raised from the tomb it will be so soaked with divine power that it will weigh much more that it weighed previously; and the man who raised [the cloth] then knows that by its good favor he has received what he requested. Many people fashion gold keys for unlocking the railings of this blessed tomb; after they present them for a blessing, the keys cure the afflictions of ill people. For an active faith overcomes all [difficulties].

In that church there are four wonderfully elegant columns that shine like snow and that are said to support the ciborium over the tomb.[30]

28. The apostle Paul.

The apostle Paul was struck with a sword and died at Rome one year later but on the same day that the apostle Peter had suffered. Milk and water flowed from his holy body. It is not surprising that milk flowed from the body of the man who had labored with and given birth to unbelievers and who had nourished them with spiritual milk and led them to solid food by explaining the obscurities of the holy Scriptures. I have heard many stories about his miracles, but I prefer to describe only one of many miracles.

In some place it happened that, at the prompting of a demon, a man readied a noose to choke out his own life. Once he discovered a hidden nook in the room where he was to do this, he wrapped the rope around a beam and began to tie the noose. But all the time he was calling upon the name of the apostle Paul, and he said: "Help me, St

---

[30] The emperor Nero reigned from 54 to 68, but the evidence for the martyrdom of Peter and Paul at Rome [*HF* I.25, *GM* 28] is not definitive, despite their later prominence as the patron saints of Rome and the papacy: see C.Pietri (1976) 357-65, 1537-71. The great church in honor of St Peter was constructed on the Vatican Hill during the mid-fourth century: see Krautheimer (1965) 32-6, and C.Pietri (1976) 51-69. In Gaul the cult of St Peter and St Paul had appeared at least by the end of the fourth century since Martin founded a church in their honor at Marmoutier [*HF* X.31]: see Ewig (1960) 19-29, and (1960a). By the later sixth century popes such as Gregory I preferred to circulate as relics items that had been sanctified by contact with saints' bodies or tombs rather than actual corporeal relics: see McCulloh (1976).

Paul!" But behold, a hideous black spirit whose likeness was similar to nothing except a demon appeared to him and urged him on by saying: "Come, come, do not delay; quickly finish what you have started." But although the man went on with his same task of choking out his life, always he cried: "Most blessed Paul, be my helper!" When the noose was finally ready, the spirit strongly urged him to put it over his neck; but suddenly another spirit, similar to the first one, appeared and said to the first spirit who was with the man: "Flee, you wretch! Behold, the apostle Paul is coming here! After being invoked by this man, behold, he is present!" Then both spirits vanished, and the man came to his senses. On his trembling chest he signed the cross of the Lord's power; his cheeks were flooded with a torrent of tears; he regretted having attempted suicide. It is therefore obvious that this same man was saved from the precipice of a harsh death by the power of this blessed apostle.

29. John the evangelist.

The apostle John, an evangelist of God, after completing the course of his prescribed struggle and the text of his teaching of salvation descended into a tomb while he was still alive and ordered that he be covered in the ground. Still today his tomb produces manna with the appearance of flour; blessed relics of this manna are sent throughout the entire world and perform cures for ill people. This is that John whom the Lord loved more than [he loved] the other apostles and who was privileged by the love of such affection that he reclined on the shoulder of the sacred body and drank in the secrets of the heavenly mysteries. For in the hour of his suffering, as he hung on the cross to save the world, our Lord entrusted his glorious mother to John as if, in a manner of speaking, to a special disciple. After his resurrection he said about John: "So I wish him to remain, until I come again" [John 21:22].

In Ephesus there is the place in which this apostle wrote the Gospel that in the church is called by his name. On the peak of this mountain there are four adjacent walls without a roof. John waited in these walls, praying earnestly and constantly beseeching the Lord on behalf of the sins of the people. It was granted to him that no storm would threaten that place until he had completed his Gospel. Even today the place is so distinguished by the Lord that no rain falls there and no violent storm comes near.

Mary Magdalene is buried in Ephesus, although there is no building over her [tomb]. In that city are also the Seven Sleepers,

concerning whom I intend, at the Lord's command, to write something
in the future.[31]   In the same city was the image of Diana that the
apostle Paul destroyed [Acts 19:23-41].   But let us return to our
original subject.

30. The tomb of the apostle Andrew.

On the day of his festival the apostle Andrew works a great
miracle, that is, [by producing both] manna with the appearance of flour
and oil with the fragrance of nectar which overflows from his tomb. In
this way the fertility of the coming year is revealed. If only a little oil
flows [from his tomb], the land will produce few crops; but if the oil
was plentiful, it signifies that the fields will produce many crops. For
they say that in some years so much oil gushed from his tomb that a
torrent flowed into the middle of the church. These events happened in
the province of Achaea, in the city of Patras where the blessed apostle
and martyr was crucified for the name of the Redeemer and ended his
present life with a glorious death.[32] But when the oil flows, it offers

---

[31] Although without giving any arguments, Gregory has here identified
John the beloved apostle as the author of the fourth Gospel. Elsewhere he
claimed that the emperor Domitian had exiled the apostle John to the island of
Patmos and that John survived the emperor's death in 96 [*HF* I.26]. This
"manna" is probably to be identified with the dust that some people thought
John pushed to the surface with his breath as he slept in his tomb: see
Augustine, *In Ioannis evangelium* 124.2 (*PL* 35.1970-1), for the story, with
Foss (1979) 33-6, 126-7. For Gregory's account of the Seven Sleepers of
Ephesus, see *GM* 94.
    [32] Later traditions claimed that Andrew, one of the original twelve apostles,
had become a missionary to Asia Minor, Scythia, Parthia, or Greece, and that he
had been martyred in Achaea. For a large collection of miracle stories about St
Andrew, see the *Liber de miraculis beati Andreae apostoli* [= *MA*], ed. M.Bonnet,
MGH, SRM 1.2 (1885) 826-46. In the preface to this collection the author
stated that he had found a book about the miracles of St Andrew that he intended
to condense into one small volume because some people had dismissed it as
apocryphal on the basis of its verbosity. Bonnet, o.c. 821-2, argued that
Gregory was the author of this condensed volume; despite lingering scepticism,
others have agreed that the *MA* is Gregory's adaptation of a fourth-century text:
see Zelzer (1977), and Prieur (1981). The book that he condensed was apparently
a Latin version of the "Acts of Andrew", an apocryphal account originally
composed probably during the second century, although Gregory deleted or
changed most of the theological implications and doctrines that later churchmen

such a strong fragrance to [people's] noses that you might think a collection of many different spices had been sprinkled there. A miracle and a blessing for the people accompany this [flow of oil]. For salves and potions are made from this oil; once used, they offer great relief to ill people. After the glorious reception of Andrew [in Paradise] many miracles are said to have been revealed either at this tomb or in various places where his relics are located. I do not think it inappropriate to relate a few of these miracles, because the edification of the church is found in the glory of martyrs and the power of saints.

In the time when king Chlodomer of the Franks was killed, an army supplied itself by devastating Burgundy,[33] where relics of the aforementioned martyr [Andrew] and of the martyr Saturninus were kept in a church. The church was set on fire, and already the bulk of the beams had collapsed. The poor people and the old people whom the barbarians had left behind wept and said: "Woe to us, who today are without the assistance of such relics. If these relics are lost, we will have no more hope for the present life." While they were weeping in this way, a man came from Tours at the command of God and shared in their grief. Once he heard about the power of the martyrs, he entered the middle of the flames, protected more by his faith than by a shield. After seizing the holy relics from the altar, he was not injured by the fire and ran outside. But suddenly he was so paralyzed that he could not walk as before. The man who was carrying the relics judged himself unworthy [to do so]; so he selected a guiltless young girl to carry the treasure. He hung the reliquary around her neck and quickly returned in this way to his mother city. The relics were placed in the altar of a

---

had found objectionable: see Hornschuh (1965). He had also read, but did not summarize, an account of Andrew's martyrdom [MA 36]. In this collection of stories Gregory repeated the miracle of the manna and oil [MA 37], and he was one of the few to record Andrew's visit to Constantinople [MA 8]; this latter legend became particularly important during the seventh century to support the claim of apostolic foundation for the see of Constantinople: see Dvornik (1958) 181-222. Gregory also mentioned that he had been born on the festival of St Andrew on November 30 and that he therefore considered himself a "foster son" of the saint [MA 38].

[33] Chlodomer had been killed in 524 during a battle against king Godomar of the Burgundians, whose brother he had had murdered in the previous year [HF III.6, GM 74].

church at Neuvy-le-Roi, where there were as yet no relics of any saints. Every year the man piously celebrated the festivals of these martyrs. After this man died, his son did not observe these festivals. When he suffered from a quartan fever for an entire year, the son vowed to construct a new church in honor of the martyrs. Once the [new] church was completed, the fever broke and he was healed.

But I think that this did not happen without the intervention of the Divinity, because on the same day that these blessed relics were transferred to this other [new] church, men carrying relics of St Vincentius lost their way and were brought to this village [of Neuvy-le-Roi]. Then, at the request of the priest they cut off a small piece of the relics [of St Vincentius] for him, which he placed in the holy altar from which he had removed the other relics.[34]

During the reign of king Theudebert Mummolus traveled to the emperor Justinian at Constantinople.[35] As he was journeying by ship, he landed at Patras, where the same apostle [Andrew] was buried. While Mummolus waited there with his entourage, he suffered from a stone in his irritated bladder. He was doubled up with various pains and burned with a fever; he lost interest in eating and drinking and awaited only the onset of death. When he realized that he was so weak and had no hope of living, he sought to write his own will. After certifying [the will] with his signature and seals, he ordered inquiries to be made whether perhaps someone might be found in the city who was trained in the art of healing and who could offer assistance to a man who was about to die. When the current bishop was asked, he replied : "How long, most beloved [brothers], will you tire yourselves with pointless effort by requesting medicine from men, when there is here a celestial doctor who has often healed the diseases of ill people, not by administering

---

[34] Neuvy-le-Roi then had two churches, the original *ecclesia* now dedicated with relics of St Vincentius, and a new *basilica* dedicated with relics of St Andrew and St Saturninus. Vieillard-Troiekouroff (1976) 193, and L.Pietri (1983) 497-8, date this new foundation to the mid-sixth century, Weidemann (1982) II:93, to the early sixth century. Saturninus had been a martyr at Toulouse [*GM* 47], Vincentius in Spain [*GM* 89].

[35] Selle-Hosbach (1974) 132, identifies this Mummolus with the Mummolenus who accompanied king Theudebert I on his military campaign into Italy in 539. King Theudebert reigned from 534 until 547, and Justinian was emperor from 527 until 565.

[medicinal] herbs but by the application of his own power?" "And who," they asked, "is this doctor?" The bishop replied: "He is Andrew, an apostle of Christ." When [his servants] reported this news to the suffering Mummolus, he asked to be brought to the tomb of the blessed [saint]. There he knelt on the pavement and earnestly prayed for what was necessary. About midnight sleep overcame everyone present. Suddenly the ill man had the urge to attempt to urinate; he nudged one of his servants and quietly asked that a pot be brought. A pot was brought out. While Mummolus was trying to urinate, he passed a huge stone which was so solid that it clanged when it fell into the pot that had been readied. After the fever and his other pain vanished, he returned to his ship a healthy man.

31. The tomb of the apostle Thomas.
    According to the history of his suffering the apostle Thomas is said to have been martyred in India. Much later his blessed body was transferred to the city that the Syrians call Edessa, and there buried. Thereafter, in that region of India where he had first been buried there are a monastery and a church that is spectacularly large and carefully decorated and constructed. In this church God revealed a great miracle. A lamp was placed there in front of the spot where he had been buried. Once lit, by divine command it burned without ceasing, day and night; no one offered the assistance of oil or a new wick. No wind blew it out, no accident extinguished it, and its brightness did not diminish. The lamp continues to burn because of the power of the apostle that is unfamiliar to men but is nevertheless associated with divine power. Theodorus, who visited the spot, told this to me.[36]

[36] Later traditions claimed that Thomas, another of the original twelve apostles, had become a missionary to Syria, Parthia, and India, where he was martyred; eventually his body was brought to Edessa, with whose conversion to Christianity he was also associated: see Segal (1970) 66, 174-6. Although some have conjectured that Gregory composed a Latin version of the martyrdom of Thomas [cf. GM 30], in fact he neither edited nor probably even read a Latin version of the apocryphal "Acts of Thomas": see Bornkamm (1965), and Zelzer (1972).

32. The power of the church to which he [Thomas] was later moved.

In the aforementioned city [of Edessa], in which I said his blessed body was buried, a great crowd of people gathered for the festival that was approaching. They came from various regions with their prayers and their business, because for thirty days there was free license for selling and buying without the payment of any customs fees. During these days, which occurred during the fifth month [July], great and uncommon blessings were offered to the people. No quarrels arose among the people, no flies landed on carcasses, no thirsty person was without water. For although on other days water [could be] drawn only from wells that were deeper than one hundred feet, now you [could] dig a little bit and find sufficient water gushing out. Without doubt the power of the apostle [Thomas] bestowed this [blessing]. Once the festival days are over, customs fees are paid to the public treasury, the flies that had been absent return, and water near the surface dries up. Then God sends a rainstorm that so thoroughly cleanses the courtyard of the church from the trash and debris that had accumulated during the festival, that you would think that no one had even walked [in the courtyard].

33. The relics of the martyr St Stephen.

Stephen was the first deacon of the holy church and the first martyr at Jerusalem, as the sacred history of the apostles relates. He was stoned to death for the holy name of Christ whom he saw at the right hand [of God] in a spiritual vision of power; he begged the mercy [of God] for his persecutors.[37]

Near Tours there is an oratory that people long ago dedicated in Stephen's name and that I ordered to be enlarged a bit. When the reconstruction was completed, we moved the altar forward, exactly as it had been before. But while we were looking in its reliquary, we found none of the holy relics that tradition claimed [to be there]. I sent one of the abbots to fetch relics of Stephen for us from the oratory of the church

---

[37] Elsewhere Gregory claimed that Stephen had been the "first of all" to follow the way of martyrdom [*HF* I.26]; but by introducing him so late in the *GM*, Gregory has here minimized his significance. The relics of St Stephen were discovered only in 415 and then brought to the West: see Clark (1982), and Hunt (1982) 211-20.

house, but I forgot to give him the key for the reliquary, which was hanging on my belt. Once the abbot arrived, he removed the seal from the cupboard but found the reliquary locked. He was uncertain about what to do or how to act. If he returned to me, it would require much time to go and come back; if he brought the entire reliquary, he knew I would be annoyed, because in it were the relics of many saints; if he did nothing, he would not obey the order he had received. Why say more? When he took the reliquary hesitantly in his hand, the bolts clicked back and he saw that it was unlocked. He gave thanks, took the relics, and with great amazement brought them to me. At God's command I transferred them [to the altar] during the celebration of mass. Many days later I returned to Tours; there I found the reliquary just as I had left it, locked and again bolted.[38]

There is a relic of the blood of this holy deacon, as is popularly claimed, in the altar of a church at Bourges. During the episcopacy of Felix a man accused his neighbors of some crime. After he had at length abused his neighbors with provocative words and had challenged them to a public hearing, it was decreed by a mandate of the leading men of the city that the neighbors would clear themselves of this crime for which they were accused by an oath. They approached the altar of the aforementioned church, raised their hands, and swore their oath. The accuser in the case insisted in a loud voice that they had perjured themselves. Suddenly his feet were jerked up, he was tossed into the air, and his head struck the pavement. To the surrounding crowd he seemed almost lifeless. Almost two hours later when he was thought to be clearly dying, he opened his eyes and confessed his misdeed; he admitted that he had unjustly harassed these men and unjustly proclaimed them to be guilty. In this way, by disclosing the innocent and exposing the guilty the power of the blessed Stephen was clearly apparent.[39]

---

[38] The location of this oratory dedicated to St Stephen is not certain: see Vieillard-Troiekouroff (1976) 357, and L.Pietri (1983) 413-4.

[39] According to Gregory, a disciple of the first missionaries to Gaul named Ursinus [GC 79] had brought Christianity to Bourges in the later third century. Leucadius [GC 90], one of the leading men of the city, offered his house as the first church; subsequently relics of St Stephen were placed in this church [HF I.31], and then moved to the new cathedral built in the mid-fifth century: see Vieillard-Troiekouroff (1976) 59-61. Felix was bishop of Bourges during the later 560s and early 570s; after his death miracles happened at his tomb [GC

At Bordeaux an old woman, stooped by old age but strengthened by the faith of a pure mind, was accustomed to bring oil and light the lamps in the churches of the saints. In order to do her job, on Saturday night she entered the church of the blessed apostle Peter. The altar of this church was situated on top of a platform. Its lower part, like a crypt, was closed off by a door; the crypt however had its own altar with relics of saints. This venerable woman piously descended into this crypt to light the lamp, as I have said; only one young girl accompanied her. While she performed her task, the approaching night covered the world in darkness. Clerics arrived, chanted the verses of the psalms, locked the door of the crypt, and left, not knowing that the woman was inside. Once she lit the lamp, the woman hurried to the door to depart. When she found the door closed, she shouted and called by name for someone who should open it for her. Because of her old age her voice was too weak to be heard through the closed door. When she realized that no one heard, he quietly knelt on the pavement and said: "Let me pray for my sins and the sins of the people to the Lord, the creator of all, until the person who ought to open the entrance of this church returns."

She stayed awake while praying; and about midnight she saw the doors open and the entire church shine with a great light. And behold, a choir of men chanting psalms entered the church. Then, after they had recited the *Gloria* in honor of the Trinity and stopped chanting psalms, she heard them talking and complaining among themselves: "The deacon St Stephen has delayed us. For we ought already to be entering other churches, but we cannot until he whom we await first arrives." As they frequently repeated this complaint, suddenly a man dressed in white arrived. The entire group of men respectfully and humbly greeted him and said: "Bless us, St Stephen, holy deacon." He returned the greeting and offered a prayer. They asked him why he had been a bit tardy in visiting the sacred shrines. He replied: "A ship faced the danger of sinking at sea; after being summoned I went and rescued [the

---

100]: see Duchesne (1894-1915) II:28. This story about the power of relics of St Stephen is one among many in the writings of Gregory that illustrate the commonness of oaths as a method for both Romans and barbarians to clear themselves of accusations [cf. *GM* 38, 52, 57, 102]: for discussion and other references, see James (1983), and Wood (1986) 14-18.

ship]. Behold, now I am here! And so that you may verify what I am saying to be true, the garment I am wearing was clearly drenched by the waves, because salt water is still dripping [from it]."

Although pressed shivering to the pavement, the woman was intently watching all these events. After the men left and the doors by divine command were again locked, the woman went to the spot where the saint had stood and carefully soaked up in a handkerchief the drops that had fallen on the pavement. She showed the handkerchief to Bertramn, who was then ruling the city [of Bordeaux] as bishop. With great joy and amazement he took it and kept it with him. Many ill people received their health from this handkerchief; the bishop himself often snipped relics from it and faithfully placed them where he consecrated churches. I learned about these events from an account by the bishop himself.[40]

34. The apostle Bartholomew.

The history of his struggle states that the apostle Bartholomew was martyred in Asia. Many years after his martyrdom another persecution troubled the Christians. The pagans saw that everyone rushed to the tomb of Bartholomew and regularly offered prayers and incense. Blinded by jealousy, the pagans stole his body and put it in a sarcophagus made of lead. As they threw the sarcophagus into the sea, they said: "No longer will you mislead our people." But the providence of God was at work in his mysterious benevolence. The lead sarcophagus was carried by the waves and floated from that land until it came to an island called Lipari. It was revealed to the Christians that they acquire the sarcophagus; having done so, they buried it and built a large church over it.

---

[40] Bertramn was a contemporary of Gregory and served as bishop of Bordeaux until 585 [*HF* VIII.22]: see Duchesne (1894-1915) II:61-2, and Weidemann (1982) I:143-4. Not only was he related to the royal family [*HF* VIII.2, IX.33], but he involved himself in politics by supporting king Chilperic [*HF* V.18] and opposing king Guntramn [*HF* VII.31, VIII.2-7]. Gregory was even thought to have accused him of being the lover of Fredegund, Chilperic's wife [*HF* V.47, 49]. It is not clear whether this *relatus* was an oral conversion with Bertramn or his written account.

Whenever Bartholomew is invoked in this church, it is obvious from the many miracles and blessings that he assists the people.[41]

35. The bishop and martyr St Clement.

As can be read in [the account of] his suffering, the martyr Clement was thrown into the sea with an anchor tied around his neck. Now, however, on the day of his festival the sea recedes three miles and offers a dry path to people who walk and travel all the way to his tomb. There people make vows, pray, and then return to shore. During one of his festivals it happened that a woman came to the shrine with her small son. After the celebration of the festival, the woman was feasting and her young son fell asleep. While all this was happening, behold, suddenly the roar of the approaching sea was heard. The woman forgot about her son and began to run to the bank with the other people. The incoming sea followed. After she came to shore, she remembered she had left her son. She wept and threw herself to the ground, crying how miserable she was and filling the shores with her laments. She ran along the edge of the banks, on the chance that someone had seen a lifeless little boy tossed up on shore. But when she found no trace, she was consoled by her relatives and led to her own home. She spent an entire year weeping and mourning. After the year went through its cycle, she came again to the festival that she had waited for; perhaps she would be able to find some trace of her little boy. Why say more? As the sea receded, she was the first to enter and the first to arrive at the tomb. After she knelt on the ground and prayed, she stood up, her cheeks moist from excessive crying. Then she turned her eyes in another direction and saw her son in the spot where she had left him asleep. He was still asleep. She thought that he was dead and approached nearer, as if to pick up a dead body. But when she saw that he was asleep and then suddenly woke up, she picked him up safe in her arms. All the people were watching. As she kissed him she asked where he had been for the past year. He said he did not

---

[41] Later traditions claimed that Bartholomew, another of the original twelve apostles, had become a missionary to India or Parthia and that he had been martyred in Armenia.

know that an entire year had passed; he thought that he had dozed in such a sweet sleep for the space of one night.[42]

36. The water of a spring brought forth by his [Clement's] power.

In a field within the territory of Limoges there was a bubbling spring that both sustained the plants of gardens with its flow and enriched the crops of fields with its stream. After canals were constructed the water was detoured to adjacent spots, so that [physical] effort might provide [a stream of water] where nature had not supplied it. The spring had such sweet water, such an overpowering flow, that you would see the vegetables and plants rejoice whenever they were watered by it. In it the favor of divine majesty was available, with the result that wherever its stream flowed shoots quickly began to grow. But once the inhabitants of the region, as if they were playing a game, had detoured the water through different places, the spring disappeared beneath the ground because of the treachery of the deceiver (as I believe). The water now appeared in small trickles about twelve stades [i.e. about one and one-half miles] away in the middle of a swamp, where it could not do any good. Immediately everyone was afraid in their minds that something unexpected was happening to the region. The local inhabitants anticipated ruin, and at the same time they wept and mourned continuously for the good fortune they had been accustomed to having. One year, then another, passed in this drought. Everything in the region that the spring had ordinarily irrigated withered from thirst. But in the third year [of the drought] a man happened to travel by and displayed relics of the blessed martyr Clement, whom I have already mentioned. He brought these relics to Aredius, a priest of Limoges and a man devout in all holiness. Day and night the [people in the] neighborhood sadly gathered around Aredius. Since they trusted his prayer that, if he petitioned the Lord, the Lord was able to restore the spring to its proper spot, Aredius said: "Beloved brothers, let us arise. If the claim of our traveler that these are the relics of the martyr

[42] Elsewhere Gregory claimed that Clement had been the third bishop of Rome and had been martyred during the reign of the emperor Trajan from 98 to 117 [*HF* I.27]. In later traditions Clement was considered an important intermediary link between the original apostles and the organized church that subsequently developed [cf. *GM* 55].

Clement is true, then it will be apparent when his power is revealed."
With the accompaniment of the chanting of psalms he went to the
[former] location of the spring. After the chanting of the psalms he
knelt in prayer and placed the holy relics in the source of the spring.
He prayed that [just as] intercession had once revealed to those
condemned in the desert the refreshing water from a split rock [Numbers
20:11], so again the intercession of Clement should recall to this spot
the water which faithful mercy had earlier granted. Immediately the
flow of water reappeared at the source, and it spewed out [so] much
water [that] it filled and overflowed the banks that had earlier contained
it. The people were impressed and gave great thanks to the Lord, who
had displayed the power of the martyr and had deigned to grant the
prayer of his faithful [servant Aredius].[43]

37. The martyr Chrysanthus.

According to the history of his suffering, after the martyr
Chrysanthus received the crown of martyrdom with the virgin Daria he
graciously performed many healings for people. For this reason a crypt
of wonderful workmanship was constructed over their tombs. The crypt
was vaulted in the manner of arches and stood on a very solid foundation. When a crowd of people gathered for his festival, an evil emperor
had a wall constructed across the entrance to the crypt to trap the people
inside and ordered that the shrine be covered by sand and rocks. A large
mound was built on top. The records of the martyr's struggle clearly
state that this is what happened. For a long time the crypt remained
buried by this covering. Finally the city of Rome discarded its idols

[43] Gregory also wrote a separate account of the miracles and the death of
Aredius, an abbot at Limoges whom he greatly admired and who died in 591 [*HF*
X.29]. With the support of his mother Pelagia [*GC* 102] Aredius had founded a
monastery at Saint-Yrieix, in the oratory of which he kept relics of St Martin
[*HF* VIII.15]: see Vieillard-Troiekouroff (1976) 277-8. One of his special skills
was dowsing for water [*HF* X.29]; but the location of this spring is unknown:
see Vieillard-Troiekouroff (1976) 353. Aredius often served as an informant for
Gregory [*GM* 41, *VJ* 41-5, *VM* 2.39, 3.24, 4.6, *VP* 17 praef., *GC* 9]. A *Vita* of
Aredius survives, composed probably during the Carolingian period: ed.
B.Krusch, *MGH*, SRM 3 (1896) 581-609.

and yielded to Christ the Lord. Already during previous years no one knew the location of this mausoleum, until the Lord Jesus revealed and exposed it. A wall divided the place; on one side the tombs of the martyrs Chrysanthus and Daria were separated, on the other side the bodies of the other saints were placed in one tomb. But the builder left an open window in this wall that had been placed in the middle, so that a panorama was available for viewing the bodies of the saints.

Some report that when the people gathered for the sacred rituals and were walled in, they had brought with them small silver pitchers fashioned from metal and filled with the wine that was presented as an offering [during the celebration] of the divine sacrifice [i.e. the Eucharist]. It is obvious that the silver is still there and that spectators can today still see it. But because the human mind is continually overcome by evil and embarrassing desires, a subdeacon who had seen the silver through the window and whom avarice overwhelmed thought to himself what he would later do. He got up during the night, entered the church of the saints, and crawled into the burial chamber through the window. Since the night was dark, he felt with his hands and found some of the pitchers. Then, although he wanted to leave with his booty, he wandered about for the entire night, but never was able to find the window through which he had entered. At daybreak, because he was self-conscious of his wrongdoing and wished to conceal his misdeeds, in accordance with the record of the Lord's pronouncement that "everyone who does evil hates the light, lest his deeds be exposed" [John 3:20], he hid himself in the corner of the burial chamber for the entire day, so no one would detect him. The next night he again searched for the entrance but could not find it; he did the same during the third night. But on the third day when he was starving, he revealed himself to the people at the window, abandoned the silver vessels, confessed his misdeed, and with great shame exited. The people who were present knew of the crime he had committed. Much later Damasus, bishop of this holy apostolic see [of Rome], learned of the deed and ordered that the window be carefully closed over. He commemorated the spot with some verses. And still today our Lord Jesus Christ is blessed by the praise of his name at this spot.[44]

---

[44] Chrysanthus (whose name Gregory spelled as Crisantus) and Daria were thought to have been martyred at Rome in the later third century. Damasus was

38. The martyr Pancratius.

Not far from a wall of this city [of Rome] is [the tomb of] the martyr Pancratius, who is a powerful avenger against perjurers. Whenever someone who suffers from madness intends to swear a false oath at the martyr's tomb, before he approaches his tomb, or rather, after he approaches all the way to the railings that are beneath the arch where the clerics usually stand and chant the psalms, immediately either he is seized by a demon or he falls to the pavement and breathes out his spirit. In consequence, whenever a man wishes to elicit a guarantee about something from someone, he sends him nowhere else except to this church, so that he might find a true [guarantee]. For some say that although many people loiter around the churches of the apostles and of the other martyrs, they go nowhere else except the church of the blessed Pancratius for this duty [of swearing oaths]. Because his harsh punishment publicly distinguishes [oaths], either listeners believe the truth or they witness the judgement of the blessed martyr against deceit.[45]

39. The martyr John.

There are many martyrs at Rome, but the histories of their suffering have not been handed down to us intact. Although a written record of the struggle of the bishop John has not come into my hands, I am unable to pass over what I heard from believers. When John became bishop, he zealously cursed heretics and dedicated their churches to catholicism. When king Theodoric [of the Ostrogoths] learned this, he was furious, because he was devoted to the Arian religion. He ordered soldiers to be sent throughout Italy who were to murder all catholics, however many they found. When the blessed John heard this, he went to the king intending to beg that this not take place. The king received him with treachery, bound him, and threw him into prison; the king

────────

bishop of Rome from 366 until 384. Among his many poems about saints is one in honor of Chrysanthus and Daria that was placed on their tomb: ed. A.Ferrua, *Epigrammata Damasiana* (1942) 187. But Damasus was not therefore necessarily responsible for the construction of the church: see C.Pietri (1976) 543-4.

[45] Pancratius (or Pancras) was thought to have been martyred in the early fourth century. His cult at Rome has left no archaeological trace: see C.Pietri (1976) 613 n.4.

said: "I will force you not to dare to complain anymore against my religion." The saint of God was thrown into prison and wounded with such tortures that not much later he breathed out his spirit. He died with glory in prison at Ravenna. But the pity of God immediately exacted vengeance from the wicked king. For the king was suddenly struck down by God, consumed by great wounds, and died. He immediately suffered the eternal burning of the flames of hell.[46]

40. The Christian who stood before a pagan who was sacrificing.

There is great value in the name Christian, if you perform in deeds what you confess in faith. For as the apostle says: "Faith without works is dead by itself" [James 2:17, 20]. Just as it is not birth in the flesh but rather faith that makes sons of Abraham, so also not only the grace of the name but works distinguish true Christians. Through this name darkness is illuminated, serpents flee, idolatry is overturned, the soothsayer is unemployed, the fortuneteller declines, and worshippers of demons are repulsed.

So our Prudentius records in his book written against the Jews. An emperor advanced to offer a loathsome sacrifice to demons. After adoring the gods and kneeling before the images, he watched the priests of these images who were sacrificing flocks of animals, whose heads had been wreathed in laurel and crushed with axes. An old priest investigated parts of the internal organs with his blood-stained hands. After he attempted to detect something divine among the fibers of the liver and the hearts of the animals, he noted that everything was confused, and he was unable to discover for certain what he wished to learn. Distraught, he cried out and said: "Alas, alas, I do not know what is happening that is thought to be hostile to our gods. For I see that our

---

[46] Although an Arian, king Theodoric of the Ostrogoths was generally quite accomodating toward the catholics in Italy. But when the eastern emperor, Justin I, began to persecute Arians, Theodoric sent John I, bishop of Rome since 523, on an embassy to Constantinople. Theodoric apparently thought that the embassy was unsuccessful, because he imprisoned John upon his return. Once John died in 526 probably as a result of illness and old age, he was nevertheless quickly seen as a martyr and associated with Boethius and others whom Theodoric had had excuted apparently for conniving with the eastern court: see Richards (1979) 109-19, and H.Chadwick (1981) 56-64. King Theodoric himself died later in 526.

gods are scattering far away and accept nothing from the sacrifices we
have prepared. The situation indicates that this is due to respect for
some gods who are usually hostile to us. It would be surprising if a
worshipper of the God Christ, who they claim was crucified, had not
compelled our gods to flee. The censers of incense are cooling, the fire
of the altar wastes away, and the sword plunged into the victims is seen
to become blunt. Look now, most sacred Augustus, for someone
washed in water and anointed with balsam; and let him immediately
depart, so that the gods whom we call might come." As he said this, as
if he had seen Christ himself threatening him for these remarks, he fell
lifeless to the ground and called upon the offended divinities. Then the
emperor himself removed his diadem and said: "Who here opposes our
divinities and supports the Christian religion? Whose forehead has been
marked with the sign of the chrism and who worships the wood of the
cross? Let there be no delay in speaking up." One of the emperor's
bodyguards came forward, threw his weapons to the ground, and said: "I
am the one whose God is Christ and who has been washed by baptism
and redeemed by the cross. I have always invoked his name while your
priests were offering to the demons these [animals] which have been set
out. Your gods fled from his name and could not stay in the place
where the name of such majesty had been invoked." After his bodyguard said this, the emperor was amazed and afraid and left the temple of
the demons. The bystanders were so afraid of God that no one followed
the emperor. Instead everyone lifted their hands and turned their eyes to
heaven and with one voice they together praised the Lord Christ. As
suppliants they prayed that he assist them. Lest this account seem
unbelievable to anyone, I have appended a few lines from the poem [of
Prudentius].

　　"Of all the emperors, however, there was one
　　whom I remember from my childhood, a powerful leader in arms,
　　a renowned lawgiver, in speech and in action
　　a man who cared for his country. But he did not care for preserving
　　[true] religion, since he loved innumerable gods.
　　He would bow his emperor's head before the feet of Minerva,
　　lick the clay sandals of Juno, grovel at the feet
　　of Hercules, and leave petitions on wax tablets at the knees of
　　　　Diana.
　　By chance an old man wearing the ritual headbands was sacrificing
　　　　to

Hecate and appeasing her with much blood. With bloodstained
    hands
he investigated the fibers still palpitating with the chill of death.
As a skilled interpreter he counted, until they stopped,
the final pulses of life in a heart that was becoming cold.
Suddenly the priest paled and cried out in the middle of the
    ceremony:
'What do I do? O great king, a greater divinity
that is unknown to me is interfering at our altars.
I see the spirits we summoned scattered at a distance.
Surely some unknown Christian young man has crept among us;
for this sort of man causes the [priestly] headband and gods' couch
to fear. Let any man who is washed and anointed depart far away.
After the ceremony has restarted, let beautiful Persephone return.'
He spoke, and he fell lifeless. As if he had seen Christ himself
threatening him by brandishing a thunderbolt,
the emperor turned pale as death and took off his diadem.
He looked at the bystanders [to see] which child of the chrism
had marked his brow with the sign of the cross
that, on his forehead, had disrupted the Persian chants.
One bodyguard out of the company of blond-haired youths,
a guardian of the imperial person, was apprehended and
did not deny. He threw away his two lances with the jeweled shafts
and confessed that he bore the sign of Christ.
The terrified priest was thrown aside. The emperor leapt up
and fled the marble chapel with no one accompanying him.
His frightened entourage forgot their master but bent their heads
back, raised their faces to heaven, and called upon Jesus."
I have included these verses in this selection to confirm what I have
described. I have shown what the name Christian and the banner of the
cross offer to those who believe by faith and do in deeds what they have
believed, as was said above.[47]

---

[47] In the late fourth and early fifth centuries Prudentius, a native of Spain,
wrote many poems in which he adapted classical conventions to Christian
themes. Since one series of poems glorified Spanish martyrs, Gregory found
them especially useful as sources [*GM* 92]. Gregory excerpted these particular
verses, although sometimes inaccurately, from Prudentius, *Apotheosis* 449-502,

41. The martyr and deacon St Laurentius.

In one place there was a church that had been dedicated with the relics and the name of the blessed Laurentius. Through the neglect of many years its roof had completely collapsed. When the inhabitants of the region wished to repair it, they went into the forest, cut and planed trees, made beams, placed them on carts, and brought them to the shrine. Once the beams were laid out on the ground for alignment, one was found to be too short. Immediately the bishop who had promoted the project felt great grief in his heart; he wept loudly and did not know what to do or where to turn. As he looked at the oak beam that was too short, he said: "O most blessed Laurentius, you who were glorified by being placed in a fire and who always cherish and assist the poor, consider my poverty, because my neediness has no resources for another [beam] to be brought here." Suddenly, to the surprise of all, the beam grew to such a length that it was necessary for a long piece to be cut off. After this task the people thought it improper to lose this blessing; so, in the belief that this beam had been touched and lengthened by the hand of the martyr, they cut the leftover piece into little splinters and often drove off various illnesses [with these splinters]. The priest Fortunatus commemorated this event with these verses:

"Laurentius, you who were burned in the life-giving flames because
    of your merit
and who returns with burning faith as a victor over the fire,
when the people restored the church with a beam that was too
    short,
the beams grew, and their precious faith grew too.
Although the log had been cut too short, it stretched itself because
    of your excellence.
To the extent it had previously been too short, it was cut
    afterwards.
The tree that was cut by axes was worthy to grow longer,
and the dry foliage learned to become longer.
When it had been cut again, it offered assistance to the people;
if a blind man approached without fear, he received his sight."

———

ed. and trans. H.J.Thomson, LCL (1949-1953) I:154-9. He based his summary in the preceding paragraph upon the same passage.

Fortunatus then wrote many more verses which I have omitted; I have recorded only these verses as the man's testimony. These events happened in Brioni, a town in Italy. I saw a man who suffered from a painful toothache receive a splinter of this beam from the bishop; as soon as he touched it to his tooth, the pain was immediately gone.

But I have decided that this must not be omitted, because after relics of this beam were saved from a fire set by the enemy a man brought them to Limoges. Although this man was often warned by a dream to bring the relics to abbot Aredius, he did not obey the command, and he, his wife, and their entire family began to feel ill. Then, compelled by circumstances, he brought the relics to the saint; soon he recovered his health and left.[48]

42. The martyr Cassianus.

During a time of persecution Cassianus, a martyr in Italy and a distinguished teacher of young boys, was handed over to a class of young boys by the judgement of the persecutors. In their thirst for the blood of their teacher the boys struck his head with their wax tablets, lacerated him with the blades of their pens, and tattooed the skin of their teacher with tiny pricks; they made him a martyr worthy of God. Still today there is such regard for his reputation that no one has ever dared to touch any of his things. If someone did so, either he would be seized by a demon or he would be overwhelmed by a sudden death; but he would not depart without some retribution.[49]

---

[48] Laurentius, a deacon at Rome, was martyred during the mid-third century [*HF* I.30] and subsequently became one of the important patron saints of Rome [*HF* VI.6, *GM* 45, 82]. Venantius Fortunatus was a contemporary of Gregory. He grew up in Italy but moved to Gaul in 566, where he wrote poems in honor of Frankish kings, magistrates, bishops, and other patrons, and a series of *Vitae* of saints. He eventually settled in Poitiers and finally served as bishop there at the end of the sixth century. Because of his respect for St Martin, who had once healed his eyes, Fortunatus also visited Tours and became a friend of Gregory: see Brennan (1985). Gregory here quoted from Fortunatus, *Carm.*IX.14.1-2, 11-18, ed. F.Leo, *MGH*, AA 4.1 (1881) 218. Aredius was another friend of Gregory [cf. *GM* 36].

[49] Gregory probably used the more extensive account of the martyrdom of Cassianus (otherwise practically unknown) in Prudentius, *Peristephanon* 9, ed. and trans. H.J.Thomson, LCL (1949-1953) II:220-9.

43. The miracles of the martyrs Agricola and Vitalis.

Agricola and Vitalis were crucified for the name of Christ at Bologna, a city in Italy. Because I have no extant history of their suffering, I have learned from an account of trustworthy men that their tombs were placed above ground. Since, as happens, many people either touched the tombs with their hands or kissed them with their lips, the custodian of the church was warned to keep impure people from the tombs. One audacious scoundrel lifted the lid from one tomb in order to steal something from the sacred ashes. After putting his head inside the tomb, he was crushed by the lid and barely freed by other people. He left in a state of confusion, for he did not deserve to acquire what he had presumptuously and rashly attempted. Later he approached the tombs of the saints with greater respect.

Another man collected the public taxes, but while he was travelling he carelessly lost a bag of money. As he approached the city [of Bologna], he realized that he had lost the public funds he was carrying. Then he kneeled before the tombs of the saints and tearfully prayed that by means of their power he might recover what he had lost; otherwise he, his wife, and their children would be reduced to captivity for this loss. As he went outside into the courtyard, he met a man who had found the money lying next to the road. During careful questioning the man said that he had found this sack of money at precisely the hour when the tax collector had requested the assistance of the martyrs.

Namatius, bishop of Clermont, piously sought relics of these martyrs so that he might put them in the cathedral that he was building. He sent one of his priests there [to Bologna]; the priest left with the favor of God and brought back what Namatius sought. As the priest was returning with his companions, they turned aside five miles from Clermont and took lodgings. They sent messengers to the bishop so that he might order them to prepare what they were to do. At daybreak the bishop instructed the citizens and with great piety hurried off with crosses and candles to meet the holy relics. When the priest suggested to him that he look at the blessed relics, if he so ordered, Namatius replied: "For me it is greater to believe these things than to see them. For so we read in the holy Scriptures, and the Lord himself judged those men to be blessed who had believed in him whom they had not seen" [cf. John 20:29]. Since the faith of this bishop was so strong, the Lord glorified his saints with his power. For as they were traveling, suddenly the sky turned dark, and behold, a heavy rainstorm fell on them. So much rain fell there that rivers were seen to run along the roads. But around the holy relics within the area of one entire iugerum [i.e. about two-thirds of an acre] not a single drop was seen to fall. As the people moved away, the rainstorm followed them at a distance, as if offering homage. The rain refreshed the people, but it never touched those carrying the relics. When the bishop saw this, he extolled the Lord who so complimented his own faith and who deigned to perform such deeds to the glory of the saints. Once his congregation assembled, with great celebration and piety bishop Namatius dedicated the holy cathedral that was distinguished by these relics.[50]

44. Victor of Milan.

At Milan the illustrious martyr Victor is honored, because often he releases bound men from prisons and allows captives to depart as free men. At one time Apollinaris was fleeing to Italy with duke Victorius, who some say was killed in Rome. The inhabitants of one region seized Apollinaris as a captive, and said: "You will not see your fatherland, but like your companion you will suffer an appropriate penalty." After making these threats they sent him into exile at Milan. But it happened that it was the time for the festival of St Victor and people were assembling. Since he was constrained without restriction by an open custody, Apollinaris attended the vigils. He knelt before the holy tomb of the saint and began to pray more fervently than always that the power of the martyr free him from this exile. As he left the church about midnight, he heard one of the beggars talking with another. The beggar said: "O fellow beggar, what do you think of the power of this martyr? I tell the truth and I am not mistaken that tonight whatever captive flees and is liberated from his master will return to his fatherland as a free man and will be pursued no further." Apollinaris took these words as a sign sent by the will of God. Again and again he knelt at the tomb of the martyr and prayed that he be

---

[50] Agricola and Vitalis were thought to have been martyred in the early fourth century, although their bodies and relics were not discovered at Bologna until 393 [*GM* 46]. Namatius was bishop of Clermont in the mid-fifth century and constructed the cathedral in the city [*HF* II.16]: see Duchesne (1894-1915) II:34. His wife built a church dedicated to St Stephen [*HF* II.17]: see Vieillard-Troiekouroff (1976) 85-9, 97-8.

helped by the martyr's power and that he be able to leave without any opposition. Next he called his servant and ordered his horse to be saddled; he said: "Today we must be freed from the chain of this captivity." After mounting their horses they crossed the peaks of the Alps that were covered with drifts of snow and reached Clermont. The power of the blessed martyr preceded them, so that no one asked where they were going or whence they had come. It is obvious that they were saved from this tribulation by the assistance of the blessed martyr.[51]

45. The broken chalice.

In the same city [of Milan] there is a church of St Laurentius the deacon, whom I have already mentioned. In the church there is a crystal chalice of marvelous beauty. But once after the celebration of mass, as a deacon was carrying the chalice to the holy altar, it slipped from his hand, fell to the ground, and was smashed into small pieces. The deacon was pale and white, but he carefully gathered the fragments of the chalice and placed them on top of the altar. He never doubted that the power of the martyr could fuse them together again. After spending the night keeping vigils, weeping, and praying, he looked for the chalice and found it on top of the altar in one piece. When this miracle was announced to the congregation, it encouraged their hearts with such devotion that they requested the bishop to celebrate another festival to God in honor of Laurentius. The chalice was hung over the altar. The bishop of the city celebrated the festival then, and directed that in the future a festival be celebrated most piously every year.

[51] This Victor was probably the African soldier thought to have been martyred at Milan in the early fourth century. Apollinaris was the son of Sidonius, who had been bishop of Clermont from c.470 into the 480s; Victorius had been appointed duke by king Euric of the Visigoths in the province of First Aquitania during the 470s, but behaved outrageously [*HF* II.20]. In c.479 both Apollinaris and Victorius fled to Italy, perhaps because of feuding between local Gallic aristocrats: see Stroheker (1948) 86-7, and *PLRE* II:114, 1162-4. After his return, Apollinaris supported king Alaric II of the Visigoths and even led a contingent of men from Clermont on his behalf in the decisive battle against king Clovis and his Franks in 507 [*HF* II.37]. Through the intervention of his wife and his sister [*GM* 64] Apollinaris eventually became bishop of Clermont in 515, but died a few months later in 516 [*HF* III.2].

46. The bodies of St Gervasius and St Protasius, and St Nazarius.

In this city [of Milan] there are the victorious bodies of the blessed martyrs Gervasius and Protasius. According to the history of their suffering, for a long time their bodies were concealed underground. Their location was revealed to the blessed Ambrose, who found the bodies. After a display of miracles, the bodies were buried in a church that Ambrose had built from his own zeal. Tours in particular has some older churches distinguished with relics of these saints, although by God's grace their relics were also scattered throughout the entire compass of Gaul.[52]

Once some monks were talking about these saints, [and wondered] why the aforementioned relics had been so thickly distributed to various places. I do not think it irrelevant to insert in this selection what I heard someone say on this matter, because it is not found in the history of their suffering. For this man said that when their glorious bodies were moved into the church, during the celebration of mass in honor of the martyrs a board fell from the vault. The board struck the heads of the martyrs and drew a flow of blood. The holy blood was collected after linen cloths, robes, and even the curtains of the church were stained with it. The blood was said to have continued flowing until linen cloths were found to soak it up. Thereafter, since so many relics [of the blood] of the martyrs were gathered, they were sent throughout the whole of Italy and Gaul. St Martin received many of these relics, as the letter of the most blessed Paulinus states.[53]

---

[52] Gervasius and Protasius were thought to have been martyred during the reign of Nero from 54 to 68. In 386 bishop Ambrose of Milan discovered the bodies of these saints whom he presented as champions against Arianism. Later he assisted in the discovery of the remains of other saints, Agricola and Vitalis at Bologna in 393 [GM 43], and Nazarius and Celsus at Milan in 395: see Homes Dudden (1935) 298-320, and Dassmann (1975).

[53] Ambrose had linked the discovery of the relics of these Milanese saints with his feuds with an imperial court that favored Arianism; in contrast, despite his early association with bishop Hilary of Poitiers [GC 2], Martin was not known for his involvement in contemporary controversies over Arianism. The "letter of Paulinus" to which Gregory appealed for verification [also in HF X.31] remains suspect, although Courcelle (1964) 286-91, identifies Paulinus of Nola [GC 108] as the author. Eustochius, bishop of Tours from 442 to 458/9, also dedicated churches with relics of St Gervasius and St Protasius [HF X.31]. The emphasis on their cult would make more sense then as a reaction against the

With regard to the bodies of Nazarius and the young boy Celsus, the text of their struggle says that they suffered in Embrun, a city in Gaul. Because of the persecution of the pagans, their bodies were buried so secretly that in the future they were forgotten. The man who narrated what I have just written about the aforementioned saints used to say that a pear tree had grown over their tombs and that a poor man kept a garden in that spot that surrounded the pear tree. But when the tree as usual produced pears at the proper season, whatever ill person who was weakened by some sickness and who picked and bit into a pear always soon recovered after his sickness left him. As a result this poor man began to make a great profit. When the martyrs revealed themselves [in a vision] and ordered the tree to be cut down, the poor man broke out in tears and would not allow the tree to be cut down. But in the man's absence the pear tree was cut down and a church of marvelous workmanship constructed. In the altar of this church relics of the blessed Genesius, a martyr at Arles, are venerated. The poor man was distinguished by such faith that eventually he deserved to become a cleric for this cathedral.[54]

47. The relics of St Saturninus.

The martyr Saturninus, according to tradition, was ordained by the disciples of the apostles and sent to Toulouse. At the instigation of the pagans he was bound to the hooves of a frisky bull and then thrown

---

expanding power of the Arian Visigoths in Gaul during the mid-fifth century: see L.Pietri (1983) 154-7, 487-93.

[54] It is not clear how Gregory came to think that Nazarius and Celsus had been martyrs at Embrun, since their bodies had been found at Milan. Gregory caused further confusion by referring to this building as both *basilica*, a church built to commemorate the tomb of the martyrs, and *ecclesia*, a term usually (but certainly not always) reserved for the bishop's cathedral in the city. Vieillard-Troiekouroff (1976) 117-118, argues that Gregory had been misled by reading an account of the martyrdom of Nazarius and Celsus that placed it wrongly at Embrun, rather than correctly at Milan. Hence this building was in fact the cathedral, constructed at the beginning of the fifth century, in which relics of Nazarius and Celsus were placed after they had been imported from Italy. Weidemann (1982) II:51 n.268, suggests instead that this was a church constructed before 395 over what people thought was the tomb of Nazarius and Celsus, and that it later served as the cathedral. Genesius had been a martyr at Arles [*GM* 67].

from the steps of the Capitol. After fracturing his skull he ended his present life.[55]

As some monks were transporting his relics into another region, the path of their journey led them to pass by the boundary of the village of Brioude, which is situated in the territory of Clermont. Since the sun was setting, they turned aside to the cottage of a poor man and requested the lodging they needed. Once the man took them in, they told him what they were delivering. Advised by human intuition and fear of God the man took the reliquary with its relics to his storeroom and set it on top of the grain that was kept in a container. At daybreak the travellers took back their relics, thanked the man, and resumed the journey they had begun. But the next night the poor man received a warning from a dream in which an old man said to him: "Do not stay in this place, because it has been sanctified by the relics of the martyr Saturninus." The man thought little of this vision; as is characteristic of rusticity he remembered nothing of these warnings. But soon he fell into misfortune. His small possessions began gradually to diminish and his wife to waste away from another illness. Why say more? Within a year he had been reduced to such poverty that he possessed nothing and could not feed or house himself as the requirements of human existence demand. After thinking to himself he said to his wife: "I have sinned before God and his saints, because I did not leave this cottage as I was warned. I know that the misfortunes we now suffer have come upon us for this reason. Now however let us obey the vision that we saw and let us remove the cottage from this place, so that we might be saved." After he tore down the cottage he built an oratory out of wooden planks. Every day he prayed in this oratory and requested the assistance of the blessed martyr. Finally his misfortunes ceased. As he put his hands to work there were such good results as a

---

[55] On the basis of information in a "History of the suffering of the martyr St Saturninus," Gregory claimed that Saturninus was one of the seven missionaries sent to Gaul in the middle of the third century and that he had been martyred at Toulouse [*HF* I.30]: see Griffe (1948) and (1959), and L.Pietri (1983) 19-22. This *Passio* may have been composed in the first half of the fifth century: see Griffe (1964-1966) I:110-5, 134-6, 148-52, 395-402.

consequence that in a short time he regained more than he had lost. These events happened within our territory [of Clermont].[56]

In order to suppress the arrogance of evil men I will not pass over what a man named Plato is reported to have said. During the reign of king Chlothar Plato visited the monastery of Saint-Sernin, in whose oratory relics of this saint [Saturninus] are kept. Because he did not receive a gift from the abbot,[57] [Plato said]: "I will make this church into a house for the king, and his horses will feed in one of its corners." He left in a rage. As he was preparing to return to the king, he was seized by a fever and three days later exhaled his spirit. He quickly descended to the underworld and left the house of God to the cult of that saint in whose name it had been first consecrated.

48. The forty-eight martyrs who suffered at Lyon.

These are the names of the forty-eight martyrs who are said to have suffered at Lyon: Vettius Epagatus, Zaccharias, Macharius, Alcipiadis, Silvius, Primus, Alpius, Vitalis, Comminius, October, Philominus, Geminus, Julia, Albina, Grata, Aemelia, Postumiana, Pompeia, Rodonae, Biblis, Quarta, Materna, Elpenipsa, Stamas. These martyrs were condemned to the wild beasts: Sanctus and Maturus, Alexander, Ponticus, Blandina. These are the martyrs who gave up their lives in prison: Arescius, Photinus, Cornelius, Zotimus, Titus, Zoticus, Julius, Aemelia, Gamnitae, Pompeia, Alumna, Mamilia, Justa, Trifimae, Antonia, and the blessed bishop Photinus. A wicked judge decreed that their holy bodies be thrown on a fire and then ordered their burned ashes to be sprinkled on the Rhone river. After his orders were carried out, the Christians were very sad that the holy relics were lost. But during the night the martyrs, standing intact and unwounded, appeared to believers in that place where they had been thrown into a fire. They turned to the men and said to them: "Let our relics be gathered from this place, because none of us died. For we have been

---

[56] This oratory was probably located at Vialle: see Vieillard-Troiekouroff (1976) 337.

[57] On the basis of this comment Weidemann (1982) I:337, suggests that this monastery had previously been exempted from paying tribute. King Chlothar reigned from 511 until 561; for the location of the monastery, see Vieillard-Troiekouroff (1976) 276.

transported from here to that repose promised us by Christ, the king of heaven, for whose name we suffered." These men reported this [vision] to the other Christians, who thanked God and were restored in their faith. They gathered the holy ashes and built a church of astounding size in honor of the martyrs.[58] They buried the sacred relics beneath the holy altar, where the martyrs revealed by their public miracles that they always live with God. The place where they suffered is called Ainay, and they are therefore called by some the martyrs of Ainay.

49. The tombs of St Irenaeus, St Epipodius, and St Alexander.

So the glorious bishop Photinus, who presided as bishop for Lyon, was perfected by martyrdom, and as a result of the merit of his noble struggle he was transported to heaven. Irenaeus, a man worthy of his predecessor's merit and holiness, succeeded as bishop and also died as a martyr. Irenaeus was buried beneath the altar in the crypt of the church of the blessed John. On one side was the tomb of Epipodius, on the other the tomb of the martyr Alexander. If ill people have faith and scrape some dust from the martyrs' tombs, immediately they are healed. In this crypt there is a great brightness, which I think indicates the merit of the martyrs.[59]

[58] According to Gregory, Christianity first appeared in Gaul at Lyon [*HF* I.18]. In 177 local authorities executed many Christians at Lyon; survivors composed an account of these martyrdoms that the Greek historian Eusebius preserved in his history of early Christianity: see Griffe (1964-1966) I:33-57, and the many essays in the commemorative volume *Les martyrs de Lyon (177). Lyon, 20-23 septembre 1977* (Paris, 1978). Gregory elsewhere claimed that he had found this information about the martyrs of Lyon by reading Eusebius [*VP* 6.1]; in fact, he had certainly read the Latin translation of Eusebius' history made by Rufinus [cf. *GM* 20]. The names of these forty-eight martyrs are problematical, in part because Gregory himself listed only forty-five: see Quentin (1921). When Gregory elsewhere referred to the martyrs of Lyon, he again insisted that Vectius Epagatus (or Vettius Epagathus) was the first [*HF* I.29]. Since his father's family claimed descent from Vettius Epagathus [*VP* 6.1, *GC* 90], Gregory's interest here was personal; some of his information may also have been part of family traditions. The location of the church dedicated to these martyrs is uncertain: see Vieillard-Troiekouroff (1976) 145-7.

[59] Before his death in the late second or early third century, Irenaeus had distinguished himself by his opposition to heresies: see Griffe (1964-1966) I:57-74. Although Gregory elsewhere repeated that Irenaeus (whose name he spelled as Hereneus or Hireneus) had been a successor to bishop Photinus of Lyon, he

50. The martyr St Benignus.

Benignus, another witness to the name of the Lord, was perfected by martyrdom in the town of Dijon. After his martyrdom, because he was buried in a huge sarcophagus, men of our time and in particular the blessed bishop Gregorius always thought that some pagan had been buried there. For the countryfolk fulfilled their vows there and quickly received what they sought. After one man noticed the many blessings there, he brought a candle to the tomb of the saint; after lighting it, he returned home. A young boy watched this, and after the man left he went down to the tomb to extinguish the burning candle and steal it. As he approached, behold, a huge serpent came from another direction and wrapped itself around the candle. The boy was afraid and turned back; even after trying a second and third time, he was unsuccessful because the serpent blocked him. Although these stories and others like them were reported to the bishop, in no way did he believe them, but all the more did he strongly encourage people not to worship there. Finally the martyr of God once revealed himself to the blessed confessor [Gregorius] and said: "What," he asked, "are you doing? Not only do you scorn this tomb, but you disdain those who honor me. Do not do this, I ask, but quickly prepare a shelter for me." Gregorius was disturbed by this vision; he went to the sacred tomb and there at length wept and begged forgiveness for his ignorance. And because the crypt that had been vaulted by the original builders was in disrepair, the blessed bishop rebuilt it and vaulted it with elegant workmanship. But for some unknown reason the holy sarcophagus remained outside. When Gregorius wished to transfer it inside, he gathered the abbots and other monks for the task. At this assembly the holy martyr performed a spectacular miracle for the people and for his own confessor Gregorius. This sarcophagus was in fact so large, as I said, that at the

---

also claimed that Irenaeus had been sent to Lyon by Polycarp, bishop of Smyrna until his martyrdom in c.155 [cf. *GM* 85], and that he had been martyred before the forty-eight martyrs [*HF* I.29]. In fact, although in the first half of the sixth century someone in Burgundy composed a *Passio* of Irenaeus, there is considerable doubt whether Irenaeus had suffered martyrdom at all: see van der Straeten (1978). Epipodius and Alexander were thought to have been martyred at the end of the second century, and Epipodius' sandal became a prized relic [*GC* 63]: see Vieillard-Troiekouroff (1976) 143-5.

time three yoke of oxen were unable to budge it. They dallied for a long time and did not figure out how to carry the sarcophagus inside. So, in the spotlight of the candles and with the accompaniment of the loud chanting of psalms, St Gregorius picked up the sarcophagus at the end with the martyr's head and two priests moved it at the foot end. Effortlessly they brought the sarcophagus into the crypt and placed it where they had decided. For the people this was a fantastic sight. A few years later the blessed confessor Gregorius acquired from men travelling to Italy a history of Benignus' suffering. Thereafter the holy martyr revealed himself to the people with many miracles. Without delay Gregorius ordered a large church to be constructed over the crypt.[60]

There is another church nearby in which the nun Paschasia is venerated. At that time it seemed to the builders that an old woman had come out of the church. She was dressed in black, her hair was white as a swan, and her face was glorious. She said to the builders: "Greetings, my most beloved men; complete your fine work. Let the scaffolding that supports this building be raised, and the task that has such a director will justly proceed quickly. For if it were possible for the sight of your eyes to see, you would surely realize that St Benignus is directing your construction." After she said this, she entered the church from which she had come and never again appeared to anyone. The men of that time thought that the blessed Paschasia had appeared there.[61]

Many people pour wine and cider into the depressions that were made on top of the stone to which Benignus' feet were affixed with

---

[60] Benignus of Dijon was most likely an apocryphal martyr whose cult Gregorius invented and about whom a *Passio* was eventually written, perhaps at the beginning of the sixth century: see Delehaye (1933) 354-5, and Griffe (1964-1966) I:138-48. Gregorius was Gregory's great-grandfather who had first served as count of Autun before becoming bishop of Langres and Dijon; upon his death in 539 or 540, his son Tetricus succeeded him as bishop. Gregory eventually wrote a longer account of the life and accomplishments of his great-grandfather [*VP* 7], after whom he was partially named. Gregory's full name was Georgius Florentius Gregorius [*GM* praef.]; the first two names came from his paternal grandfather and father respectively, the third (by which he is now known) from bishop Gregorius: see Krusch (1951) IX.

[61] Paschasia is otherwise unknown. Gregory retold this story about her appearance to the builders more briefly in *GC* 42.

molten lead. Then, once eyes afflicted with inflammation or some other sores are soaked [with this liquid], immediately the illness leaves and they are healed. I certainly experienced this. For when my eyes were severely inflamed, I was touched with this holy ointment and immediately lost the pain.

When that plague of the groin that the prayer of the bishop St Gallus [eventually] repulsed was approaching the territory of Clermont, signs and marks appeared on the walls of homes and churches suddenly, as men looked. My mother had a vision during the night in which it seemed that the wine that was in our cellars had been changed into blood. She wept and said: "Woe am I, because my house has been marked for the plague." A man replied to her and said: "Do you know that the [anniversary of the] suffering of the martyr Benignus will be celebrated tomorrow on the Kalends of November [November 1]?" "I know," my mother said. He said: "Go, keep the vigil in his honor during the entire night, celebrate mass, and you will be rescued from the plague." My mother awoke from her sleep and did what she had been ordered. Although the houses of our neighbors were marked, our home remained untouched.[62]

51. The relics of the martyr St Symphorianus.

The martyr Symphorianus consummated his martyrdom at Autun. At the spot where he had been struck with a sword and where his blood flowed, a monk picked up three small stones [stained] with his blood. He put the stones in a silver reliquary and put the reliquary in the holy altar of a church that was constructed with wooden planks at Thiers, a village [in the territory] of Clermont. At the time when king Theuderic of the Franks invaded the region, the enemy devastated this village with fire. The house of God, which, as we have said, was constructed of

---

[62] Throughout the later sixth century the plague appeared at intervals in western Europe: see Biraben and Le Goff (1975). In 543 the plague threatened Gaul, perhaps for the first time. Since Gregory was then only a young boy, he would have heard about the plague from his parents or perhaps directly from his uncle Gallus, who was bishop of Clermont from 525 until 551 and who was successful at warding off the plague [VP 6.6]. After Gallus' prayers were effective, signs appeared on the walls of buildings; the people called these signs "Tau", presumably because they were similar to the Greek letter *tau* whose shape resembled a cross [HF IV.5].

wood planks, caught fire from the other houses that were burning and was destroyed. The people wept and said: "If only the holy relics have not perished!" The fire had left a huge pile of live coals. Suddenly a north wind began to blow and fan the flames, and the embers left in the fire were forcibly and widely scattered. Behold, the silver reliquary was intact in the middle of a burning fire, and it seemed to glisten like a shining star. The clerics who were there at the time picked it up; after looking, they found that none of the holy relics was broken and that this tiny ornament had been preserved in a blaze so hot that it could have quickly melted, so to speak, not only these relics but even a thousand pounds of silver or iron. Truly a great miracle appeared there that encouraged people to worship God and honor his name. After they built another church on the same spot, the people placed these holy relics in the altar.[63]

52. The martyr St Marcellus.
Concerning the miracles of the blessed martyr Marcellus of Chalon-sur-Saône, a few traditions worthy of memory have been transmitted to me. Although these memorials may seem insignificant in the telling, they must be recounted in honor of him who works these miracles in individual cases. For some reason Fedamius, the son of a former priest at Clermont named Eunomius, went to Chalon-sur-Saône. He lodged at the church of the martyr St Marcellus [at Saint-Marcel-lès-Chalon], where he received a stipend for his upkeep from the abbot of the place. He told this story which I repeat. He said: "A dispute arose between two men. They went to court, but the lawsuit came to this, that they resolve it with an oath. They entered the church of the holy martyr. One man raised his hands to take the oath. Even though he

---

[63] Symphorianus was thought to have been a martyr of the mid-third century, less likely of the late second century: see Griffe (1964-1966) I:152-3, 160. In the middle of the fifth century a priest at Autun constructed a church dedicated to St Symphorianus [*HF* II.15]; the saint's *Passio* may also have been written, or rewritten, at the same time [*GC* 76]: see Vieillard-Troiekouroff (1976) 44-5. People also celebrated the cult of St Symphorianus at Tours, where bishop Perpetuus had prescribed vigils before his festival day [*HF* X.31], and at Brioude near Clermont [*VJ* 30]. King Theuderic invaded the Auvergne in c.524/5 because a local aristocrat had previously attempted to betray Clermont to a rival king [*HF* III.9, 12-13, *VJ* 13, 23, and the note to *GM* 64].

had his mouth open and intended to pronounce the name of the saint, the word stuck in his throat and his tongue could not be flexed for speaking. But lest this seem to be too minor for the glorification of the blessed athlete, the man, with his hands still raised, stiffened up as if [he were] completely made of bronze. Once a prayer was offered on his behalf, it secured freedom for this man who had been bound by the wiles of the devil. After his release he confessed his misdeed in his own words, and he changed what he had wrongly done."[64]

53. The martyr St Valerianus, his [Marcellus'] companion.

The blessed athlete Valerianus is linked with this martyr [Marcellus], to whom he was related both by blood and by his struggle. After Valerianus consummated his struggle he was buried in the village of Tournus, forty miles from Chalon-sur-Saône. Then Gallus, the count of Chalon-sur-Saône, was ill with the pain of a bowel disease. This disease not only tortured his whole stomach, but it also flared up with such a tumor that he was thought to be dropsical. He was unable to eat or drink anything; in addition to his disease he was becoming weak from the affliction of starvation. When he was nearly lifeless and knew he was without hope, he asked to be brought to the tomb of the blessed martyr. After he was brought there, he was approached by the priest Epyrechius, a virtuous man who was then in charge of the church and who was a man with a pure mind, as I have seen with my own eyes. Epyrechius said to the count: "If you wish to be cured, trust in the power of the glorious martyr and vow that you will send one beam and its fittings for the repair of the roof of this church. You will acquire his support if you piously perform what you promise." The count prayed fervently and vowed what the priest had suggested. Immediately he was healed. Without anyone reminding him he ordered the beam to be brought to the church of the saint. Behold what the Lord Jesus reveals on earth in the holy martyrs whom he has glorified and received in the heavenly kingdoms! And deservedly so, because they believed his holy name in their hearts, called upon it in their works, and confessed it in their trials. Not only did they follow their

---

[64] Little of historical veracity can be said about the martyr Marcellus: see Griffe (1964-1966) I:143, 160. In 587 a man tried to assassinate king Guntramn in this church [HF IX.3]: see Vieillard-Troiekouroff (1976) 264-5.

Lord as faithful servants, but with themselves as examples they stimulated others to follow.[65]

54. Timotheus and Apollinaris.

Timotheus and Apollinaris consummated their martyrdom in Rheims and deserved [to enter] the heavenly kingdoms. After building a church in their honor, a pious man sought relics of these martyrs. The current bishop arranged for a priest [to convey the relics] with honor. As the priest was travelling, a brash and, I think, properly unworthy woman advanced down the road, greeted the priest, and kissed the linen cloth that covered the holy ashes. She asked that some of these relics be given to her. The priest hesitated for a long time and postponed giving [anything to her]. Finally he was overcome by her insistence and cut off a small piece for her. He mounted his horse and began to resume the journey that had been entrusted to him. But even though he spurred both flanks of his horse, he could not be moved forward at all; in fact, he was so weighed down that he could scarcely lift his head. The priest realized that he was bound by the power of the martyr. Motivated by remorse, he quickly retrieved what he had under the influence of negligence presumed to distribute. Once he returned to the reliquary the relic he had given away, he was allowed to proceed.[66]

55. The martyr Eutropis.

Eutropis, a martyr of Saintes, is said to have been sent to Gaul by the blessed bishop Clement, who also consecrated him with the grace of the episcopal order. Since Eutropis fulfilled the duty of this office by preaching to unbelievers, the pagans whom the instigator of envy did not allow to believe rose against him. After his head was crushed, Eutropis died as a victor. But because at that time a persecution was

---

[65] The historical existence of Valerianus is as uncertain as that of Marcellus: see Griffe (1964-1966) I:144, 160. Gallus and his magistracy cannot be dated: see Selle-Hosbach (1974) 97.

[66] Timotheus was thought to have been a martyr at Rome in the early fourth century, and Apollinaris was the first bishop of Ravenna and thought to have been martyred in the mid- or later first century. Somehow, perhaps because of the presence of their relics, they had come to be considered martyrs of Rheims: see Delehaye (1933) 361, and Griffe (1964-1966) I:140. The current bishop remains unidentified.

raging, he was not buried in a proper place and he was not venerated with the accustomed honor by the Christians. The fact that he had been a martyr was completely forgotten. It is said that his martyrdom was revealed in this manner. Many years later a church was built in his honor. At the completion of the construction Palladius, who then governed the seat of the episcopal order, gathered the abbots and requested that the sacred ashes be transferred to the spot he had prepared. When this was accomplished, two abbots lifted the top [of the tomb], looked at the holy body, and noticed a scar on Eutropis' head where the blade of the axe had struck. But lest this current observation be misunderstood, spiritual instruction taught the same. While the clerics were stretching out their limbs in sleep during the following night, Eutropis appeared to these two abbots in a vision and said: "Be aware that I consummated my martyrdom with that scar that you saw on my head." Thereafter the people knew that he was a martyr, although there was no written account of his suffering.[67]

56. The martyr Amarandus.

Amarandus, a martyr of Albi, was buried after completing the course of a faithful struggle; but he lives in glory. As the history of his suffering states, for a long time his tomb was covered by brambles and concealed beneath thorn bushes. But at the command of the Lord it was revealed to the Christians, and the crypt in which he was buried was uncovered and shone forth. Then, because of the outbreak of hostility, the residents abandoned this place. [New] inhabitants came

---

[67] Clement was one of the first bishops at Rome and was linked directly with the original apostles [*HF* I.27, *GM* 35]; even though it is most unlikely that he had sent a missionary to Gaul, legends about the Clementine origins of some Gallic churches became common during the sixth century: see Griffe (1955), and Gilliard (1975). Eutropis (or Eutropius) was thought to have been the first bishop of Saintes. Bishop Palladius of Saintes was a contemporary of Gregory [*GC* 56, 59]: see Weidemann (1983) I:193-4. They had once met in 585 [*HF* VIII.2, 7], and in 589 Palladius acquired some relics of St Martin from Gregory [*VM* 4.8]. Since he promoted the cult of St Eutropius by constructing a new church, Palladius may also have fabricated this story about the saint's association with Clement and his martyrdom as an explanation for the scar on his head: see Griffe (1964-1966) I:108-9, 142, and Vieillard-Troiekouroff (1976) 281-3.

from far away and attempted to offer honor to the blessed martyr as if to their own guardian. Since therefore Christians frequently and piously brought candles, one day it happened that the length of his journey prevented a man from bringing a small flame with which to light his candle. In order to produce a spark he struck a piece of iron against a flint he had picked up. While he did this, striking the flint with repeated blows, he was unable to strike a spark; but the candle that was already placed on the holy tomb was lit by a heavenly torch. It happened that what the labors of men did not achieve was accomplished by the majesty of the divine name. Once human effort ceased, the ceremonies of heaven were performed and the burning candle was bright in the gleam of a new light. When the people saw this, no one again dared to bring a small flame for lighting a candle. Later more men began to settle in this place. And once there were houses in which a fire burned, this miracle was no longer offered to people, although the spot is frequently honored with other miracles.[68]

57. The martyr Eugenius.

Eugenius, a martyr during the persecution of Huniric, was buried in this crypt. The account of the suffering of Eugenius and his companions relates that this great ornament of the episcopal honor was sent into exile at Albi. Although he was noted in this world for his great miracles and had already triumphed as a victor over the torments of martyrdom, through the Lord's revelation he learned the moment of his calling when he would be summoned to glory. In particular, that which was unknown to the people had been revealed to him. Knowing that he would be a companion of the martyr Amarandus, he went to his tomb, knelt on the ground, and for a long time prayed to the Lord. Then, with his arms spread out over the pavement, he sent his spirit to heaven. The Christians picked him up and ordered his body to be buried in the crypt I have already mentioned.[69]

[68] Amarandus and his cult might be another invention of the sixth century: see Griffe (1964-1966) I:142. The crypt with his tomb was at Vieux: see Vieillard-Troiekouroff (1976) 340-1.

[69] Gregory was again confused about the past history of the Vandals. In 429 they had crossed from Spain to North Africa. In 477 Huniric had succeeded his father Geiseric [*GM* 12]; he reigned as king of the Vandals until 484.

At a certain time when many people have gathered for his festival, much business takes place in the courtyard. A girl, one of the inhabitants of the region, went to a stall as if intending to buy something. When she saw an ornament she liked, she took it from the merchant. Immediately, more swiftly than words [can say], she gave the ornament to someone else and then claimed that she had not received it. But the merchant insisted: "I offered it to you with my hand, and you took it for a closer inspection." When the girl denied [the accusation], the merchant said: "If, under the influence of greed, you so persist in denying, the blessed martyr Eugenius will judge. If you take an oath before his tomb and say that you did not receive the ornament, then I will think that what I misplaced was not a loss." Promising that she could be cleared by this oath, she quickly went to the tomb. When she raised her hands to swear her oath, immediately she lost control of her limbs and became stiff. Her feet were glued to the pavement, her voice stuck in her throat, and her mouth hung open without any words. The merchant and the other people saw this, and he said: "Young girl, let the ornament that you took from me be of use to you. The punishment given by the martyr is sufficient." After saying this, he left the place. For a long time the girl was held in this pain. Finally, at the martyr's command, she spoke and openly confessed what she had wished to conceal in secret. What are you doing, o accursed greed? Why do you, female (but not male) mind, succumb to seeking after others' possessions? Why do you pierce the sturdy breastplate of the mind with the small arrow of cupidity? Why, o mankind, do you accumulate talents of rusty gold with which you will burn in hell? What is the use to you of money that will perish and that poses a threat to eternal life, according to that saying of the Lord: "What does it profit a man if he gains the whole world but suffers the loss of his life? Or what will a man exchange for his own life?" [Matthew 16:26].

Having read the *Passiones* of various martyrs Gregory emphasized Huniric's reputation for persecuting catholic Christians: "men cannot comprehend how many Christians were killed during his reign on behalf of the most holy name of Christ" [*HF* II.3]. Eugenius became bishop of Carthage in c.480; he may have been persecuted by king Huniric [*HF* II.3], but he first went into exile elsewhere in North Africa from 484 until 487, and then again during the reign of king Thrasamund in c.502 to Albi, where he died in 505: see Courtois (1955) 262-5, 293-304.

58. The church at Yzeures in the territory of Tours.

In the village of Yzeures, within the territory of Tours, there is a church that is distinguished by many holy miracles. The church has the usual windows that are covered by glass in a wood frame. The windows hence more clearly offer to the holy church the light that the world deserves. A bold thief came to this church and entered it at night. When he realized that everything was watched by custodians and did not notice any holy vessels that he might steal, he said to himself: "If I cannot find something, I will steal these glass windows that I see. After melting the metal, I will acquire some gold for myself." Then, after stealing and breaking the glass windows, he took the metal and came to a village in the territory of Bourges. He put the glass in a furnace and heated it for three days, but he accomplished nothing. [Although] he was overwhelmed by his crime and [although] he realized that a divine judgement had been passed on him, he was not upset and persisted in his evil deeds. He took from the furnace glass that had been changed into some sort of small strands and sold it to merchants who had arrived. Just like a new Gehazi, once he received the money he came down with incurable leprosy [cf. II Kings 5:19-27]. For when the first anniversary of his theft was approaching, a tumor grew on his head and his eyes so swelled up that they were thought to have been torn from their sockets. Every year the same thing happened to the man on the day when he performed his theft. The wretch mourned for the glass that he could not recall from the journey on which he had sent it.[70]

59. The miracles of the confessors St Rogatianus, St Donatus and St Similinus.

At Nantes two martyrs had been murdered for the name of Christ. One was named Rogatianus, the other Donatus. At Nantes there is also a great confessor named Similinus. During the reign of king Clovis barbarians surrounded and besieged the aforementioned city. When already sixty days had passed in this hardship, in about the middle of the night men dressed in white appeared to the people. The men were carrying burning candles and came from the church of the holy martyrs.

---

[70] Eustochius, bishop of Tours from 442 until 458/9, had founded this church at Yzeures [*HF* X.31]: see Vieillard-Troiekouroff (1976) 345.

And behold, another chorus similar to the first one proceeded from the church of bishop Similinus. The choruses joined together, greeted each other, bowed in prayer, and then returned each to the place from which it had set out. Immediately the entire enemy army was struck with great terror, and it left the region so quickly that at dawn no enemy could be found. The aforementioned miracle had appeared to Chillo, the commander of this army. He had not yet been reborn by the water and the Holy Spirit; but he was immediately stung in his heart and turned to the Lord. After being reborn by a second birth, in a loud voice he declared that Christ was the son of the living God.[71]

60. The martyr Nazarius.

There are relics of the blessed Nazarius within the territory of Nantes in a village [Saint-Nazaire] on the bank of the Loire river. Once a pious man placed on the altar of this church a belt that had been most carefully crafted out of pure gold and its fittings. He prayed that the power of the martyr might deign to assist in his affairs. After he left, a man named Britto, the most influential of the retainers of count Waroch of Brittany, came, forcibly seized the fittings of the belt, and then coveted the belt itself. A priest resisted and said: "These things belong to God and were presented to the holy martyr to assist the poor, so that those who serve with faithful devotion at this church do not suffer terrible hunger. Rather than removing them, you ought instead to present something here." The speech of this abbot did not soften the heart of this greedy man. Instead, all the more aroused he began to threaten him and said: "If you do not immediately hand over the belt, you will die by my hand." The abbot was overwhelmed and placed the ornamented [belt] on the altar in which the holy relics were kept. He said: "Here is the worthless object that you covet. If you have no fear for the power of the martyr, take it. If you dare to take it, we believe

[71] Rogatianus and Donatus were thought to have been martyred at the beginning of the fourth century, but the evidence is dubious: see Griffe (1964-1966) I:155, 163. Gregory himself was apparently not well informed, since his heading to the chapter describes them as confessors, but the chapter as martyrs. Similinus (or Similianus) had been bishop of Nantes in the mid-fourth century: see Duchesne (1894-1915) II:365. Clovis had been king of the Franks from 481/2 until 511; but it is not clear whether Chillo was commanding Franks, Saxons, or Bretons [cf. *GM* 60]: see Heinzelmann (1982) 580.

that the martyr will be a judge on your heels." But Britto had no fear and took the belt. He ordered his horse to be saddled in front of the porch of the church. The priest said to him: "No one has ever dared to mount a horse in that spot. I ask you, give glory to God and honor the martyr, so that you do not suffer any misfortune." Britto ignored the advice of the priest and mounted his horse within the holy courtyard. But when he came to leave, he struck the top of his head on the lintel of the gate and fell to the ground with a fractured skull. He was carried off by his servants and brought into the nearby cottage of a poor man; immediately he died. When Waroch heard of this, he was shaken with fear, restored the things that Britto had taken, and made many donations from his own possessions.[72]

61. The Golden Saints at Cologne.

At Cologne there is a church in which the fifty men from the holy Theban Legion are said to have consummated their martyrdom for the name of Christ. And because the church, with its wonderful construction and mosaics, shines as if somehow gilded, the inhabitants prefer to call it the "Church of the Golden Saints". Once Eberigisilus, who was at the time bishop of Cologne, was racked with severe pains in half of his head. He was then in a villa near a village. Severely weakened by this pain, as I said, he sent his deacon to the church of the saints. Since there was said to be in the middle of this church a pit into which the saints were thrown together after their martyrdom, the deacon collected some dust there and brought it to the bishop. As soon as the dust touched Eberigisilus' head, immediately all pain was gone.[73]

---

[72] Nazarius had been a martyr at Milan [GM 46]; this church was located at Saint-Nazaire: see Vieillard-Troiekouroff (1976) 269-70. The four counts of Brittany each controlled small "kingdoms" that were usually independent of Frankish control [HF IV.4]: see James (1982) 33-5, and Weidemann (1982) I:80-6. While count from 577 until c.594 Waroch frequently attempted to expand his authority over cities to the east. He invaded the territory of Nantes in 579 [HF V.31], in 588 [HF IX.18, 24], and in 590 [HF X.9]: see Selle-Hosbach (1974) 168-9. Secular abbots, who were also sometimes clerics, were responsible for the administration of some large churches and their property [cf. GM 52]: see L.Pietri (1983a).

[73] Legends about the Theban Legion claimed that Christians from Thebes in Upper Egypt were recruited into the Roman army and then stationed in the Alps.

62. The martyr Mallosus.

Bishop Eberigisilus discovered the body of the martyr St Mallosus in this way. Although it was reported that Mallosus had consummated his martyrdom in the village of Birten, men were uncertain where he had been buried. There was, however, an oratory there, in which his name was invoked. The aforementioned bishop Eberigisilus built a church in honor of Mallosus so that whenever he received some revelation about the martyr he might, with the Lord's approval, transfer his holy body to the church. Finally, in the side of the church, that is, in the wall which was next to the oratory he built an arch and included the oratory in an apse.[74] He beseeched the pity of the Lord that he reveal whatever he might order concerning the martyr. Later a deacon at Metz was guided by a vision and learned where the martyr was buried. A short time later he came to bishop Eberigisilus. Although he had never been there before, it was as if he were reciting familiar landmarks that he had seen in his vision. He said to the bishop: "Dig here, and you will find the body of the saint," that is, in the middle of the apse. When the bishop had dug about seven feet down, the scent of an overpowering perfume reached his nose and he said: "Since this sweet fragrance surrounds me, I believe in Christ, because he has revealed his martyr to me." Digging further, he found that the holy body was intact. In a loud voice he cried out, "Glory to God in the highest," and he had the entire clergy chant psalms with him. After singing a hymn he transferred the holy body to the church, and with the conventional

---

When this legion refused to support the pagan emperor Maximian at the end of the third century, its members were finally all executed. Already in the fifth century the cult of the Theban Legion had spread into Gaul: see Eucher of Lyon, *Passio Acaunensium martyrum*, ed. C.Wotke, *CSEL* 31 (1894) 165-72. One of the legion's leaders was St Mauricius (Maurice) [*GM* 74-75]: see van Berchem (1956), and Dupraz (1961). Bishop Eberigisilus (or Eberegiselus) was a contemporary of Gregory [*HF* X.15] and also discovered a martyr cult [*GM* 62].

[74] See Bonnet (1890) 749 n.1, who suggested a lacuna in the text, and Krusch (1920) 733, for a better text: "denique in latere basilicae, id est in pariete qui a parte erat oratorii arcum volvit ipsumque oratorium in absida collegit."

laudations he buried it. Some say that the martyr Victor is also buried there, but we still do not know any revelation about his tomb.[75]

63. The martyr Patroclus.

The martyr Patroclus is said to have been buried in Troyes. By his many miracles he often shows that he is a friend of God. Over his tomb was a small oratory where only one cleric served. The men of that region showed little respect for the martyr, because no account of his suffering was at hand. For it was the custom of untutored men to venerate more carefully those saints of God whose struggles they could read about. Then a man arrived from a long journey and brought a small book [with an account] of Patroclus' struggle. He presented this book for the lector, who I said served at this shrine, to read. After quickly reading it the lector was very happy; during the night, with the assistance of a lamp, he rapidly copied the book. After the men left, he showed what he had discovered to his bishop, thinking that in this way he would acquire the goodwill of the bishop. But the bishop did not acknowledge the book and thought it was instead a forgery. After striking and rebuking the cleric, the bishop ordered him to leave and said: "It is obvious that you have dictated these things in accordance with your vow [of service at the shrine]; for you never found these things from any man." But so that the power of the martyr would not be concealed, many years later an army marched into Italy; it brought back an account of the suffering of Patroclus, just as it had been written down by the cleric. The bishop was then very upset and realized that what the cleric had said was true. Thereafter, however, the people began to give more honor to the martyr. After constructing a church over his tomb [at Saint-Parres-au-Tertre], they piously celebrated his festival every year.[76]

[75] Mallosus and Victor are otherwise unknown; for their oratory and church, see Vieillard-Troiekouroff (1976) 343-4.

[76] Patroclus was thought to have been martyred during the later third century but might well be apocryphal. A *Passio* about his martyrdom was not composed until the mid-sixth century: see van der Straeten (1960), Griffe (1964-1966) I:142, and Vieillard-Troiekouroff (1976) 270-1.

64. The church of the martyr St Antolianus.

The martyr Antolianus consummated his martyrdom at Clermont. Alchima, the sister of bishop Apollinaris, and Placidina, his wife, wished to build a church in his honor. While laying the foundations they removed the bodies of many saints; for they did not know the merits of the people whose tombs they found. Because of the large number of other tombs that had filled the area from long ago, they were unable to rebury these bodies in separate graves. So they threw the bones they had collected in one pile and covered the trench with dirt. In a vision a man learned that this was not acceptable to God or to the holy martyr. The man saw the blessed Antolianus lamenting with the other saints and saying: "Woe am I, because many of my brothers have been wrongly treated because of me. But I say that those who have begun this project will be unable to bring it to completion." And so it turned out. After they constructed walls above the altar of the church, they erected a dome with curved arches on columns of Parian marble and Heraclean stone. On the vault they painted a wonderful fresco, depicted in many different colors.

This was an elegant building, but so delicate that after many years it was split by many cracks and seemed almost on the verge of collapse. Bishop Avitus recognized the problem. After foreseeing the collapse of the columns he ordered the beams, the laths, and the tiles to be removed. During the process of removal the columns received no reinforcement. When, by the will of God, the builders had climbed down from the scaffolding to eat some food and everyone else had left the church, the columns around and above the altar collapsed with a loud crash because of the immense weight on them. A cloud of dust from the crushed plaster filled the building. The bishop was pale [worrying] about the damage from two [possible] disasters, and hoped that the marble was not cracked and that no one of the congregation was dead. He did not know what disaster had happened. No one could approach the church because of the cloud of dust. Two hours later when the cloud dispersed, they entered, either to find the bodies of the dead or to investigate the ruins of the columns. They discovered that no one had died. The altar seemed to be intact; even though the columns had fallen on it from such a height, they bore no mark. Why say more? They found everything in one piece and noticed that everything had been preserved. They glorified the martyr and noted the power of God who had thus preserved the altar and the columns intact.[77]

In the territory of Clermont the martyr Julian fought for and deservedly earned a reward for his struggle. I have publicized the great deeds he performed that have been transmitted to me in a book [the *VJ*] that I dared to write about his particular miracles.[78]

65. The oratory at Yssac-la-Tourette in the territory of Clermont, where St Saturninus is buried.

At the time when Chramn came to Clermont, members of his retinue committed various crimes also in the territory of the city. Five men furtively approached the holy oratory on the estate at Yssac-la-Tourette that contained relics of St Saturninus. After breaking in, they stole the robes and other vessels for celebrating the liturgy. Under the cover of night they left. A priest recognized the theft. He searched among the local inhabitants but found no trace of the items that had been stolen. The thieves who had committed the crime quickly crossed

[77] Antolianus, whom Gregory linked with the martyr Liminius [*GC* 35], was thought to have been martyred during the third century [*HF* I.32-3]. Despite Apollinaris' checkered past [*GM* 44], Alcima and Placidina had schemed for him to become bishop in 515, although he soon died in 516 [*HF* III.2]. They perhaps initiated construction of their church of St Antolianus during his brief episcopacy: see Vieillard-Troiekouroff (1976) 94-5. Since this structure did not collapse until the episcopacy of Avitus from 571 to 594 [*GM* 66], Gregory certainly saw it during his youth. But his description here is typically imprecise; Dalton (1927) II:505, suggests that the women had a ciborium erected over the altar. A decade after his episcopacy the family of Apollinaris was in decline. After his son Arcadius failed in his attempt to hand over control of Clermont from king Theuderic to king Childebert in c.524/5 [*GM* 51], Alcima and Placidina fled to Cahors, but were captured, deprived of their property, and sent into exile [*HF* III.9, 12]: see Heinzelmann (1982) 559, and Wood (1983) 37-9, who speculates that bishop Avitus was also related to this family.
[78] Julian was thought to have been martyred at some unknown time in Brioude, a town in the Auvergne: see the anonymous *Passio S. Iuliani martyris*, ed. B.Krusch, *MGH*, SRM 1.2 (1885) 879-81. Gregory grew up in Clermont, and every year his family had attended the saint's festival at Brioude [*VJ* 24-5]. Gregory therefore considered himself to be a foster-son of St Julian [*VJ* 2, 50]. During the 580s he composed a collection of miracle stories about the saint, the *VJ*: see Monod (1872) 42-4, and Krusch (1885) 452.

into the territory of Orléans. After dividing their spoils, each accepted his portion. But as divine vengeance pursued them, soon four were killed in brawls. As the sole survivor the fifth thief claimed as his legacy the whole of their stolen goods. But once he brought everything to his house, immediately his eyes were encrusted with blood and he was blinded. Goaded by his pains and by divine inspiration he took a vow and said: "If God will notice my misery and will restore my vision, I will return what I stole to that holy place." While weeping and praying for this he received his sight. As he was traveling to Orléans he met, by God's providence, a deacon from Clermont. He handed the stolen goods to him and humbly prayed that he return them to the oratory. The deacon piously fulfilled his wish.[79]

66. St Genesius of Clermont.

Very recently, within the territory of Clermont where it borders the town of Thiers, St Genesius revealed himself at this place in this way. A poor man lost the oxen that he owned for plowing the land and that had by chance vanished from his sight. Although he looked and searched carefully, he could not find them. On the following night a man appeared to him in a vision and said: "Go on the path that leads to the forest, and you will find the oxen that you earnestly seek eating the thick grass next to a marble tombstone. After you hitch the oxen to a wagon, take the marble stone and place it on the tomb which is next to the path. For I who say this to you am Genesius, and this is my tomb. While clothed in the white robes [of someone recently baptized] I left this world as a martyr." The man got up at dawn, found the oxen next to the tombstone, and did just as he had been instructed in the vision. But a miracle also occurred on this occasion, because only two oxen moved this huge stone that many teams of oxen could hardly move. Thereafter many ill people came there, performed the requirements of their vows, and received their health. Once bishop Avitus of Clermont

---

[79] Saturninus had been a martyr at Toulouse [*GM* 47]. Chramn was a son of king Chlothar who delegated him to protect his interests in the Auvergne. There Chramn threatened bishop Cautinus of Clermont and had no regard for churches or shrines [*HF* IV.13, 16]. Eventually he conspired with his uncle, king Childebert, against his father, who finally defeated him and had him killed in 560 [*HF* IV.20].

heard of these cures, he built and dedicated a large church over the tomb of the saint. He ordered that a festival be celebrated in the church. Now large crowds of people gather in the church with their vows, as I said, and depart with their health. Avitus also distinguished this church with relics of St Genesius of Arles.[80]

67. The martyr Genesius of Arles.

This martyr Genesius, because of the strength of the fervor of his faith, consummated his struggle for the name of Christ by having his head cut off in the same city, that is, Arles. At the spot where he is said to have been beheaded there is a mulberry tree that with the assistance of the martyr often offered many benefits to ill people. But with the passage of time, after many people had broken off its branches and bark for healing purposes, it withered. What remains of the trunk is, however, still alive for those who make devout requests, and it offers similar remedies.[81]

68. The bridge over the Rhone river.

Over the Rhone river there is a bridge at the spot where the blessed martyr [Genesius] is said to have [escaped by] swimming. This bridge was placed on top of boats. Once, on the festival of the saint, it broke its anchor chains and began to swing. Because of the great weight of the people the boats broke and submerged the people in the riverbed. Everyone was placed in the same danger, and they shouted with one

---

[80] Genesius of Thiers is otherwise unknown and was perhaps an apocryphal martyr. Avitus had once taught Gregory [*VP* 2 praef.]. During his episcopacy of Clermont from 571 until 594 [*HF* IV.35], he may well have invented this cult as a local double of the cult of the better known Genesius of Arles, whose relics he also placed in this church [cf. *GM* 73, for another double]: see Griffe (1964-1966) I:140, and Vieillard-Troiekouroff (1976) 293-4.

[81] Genesius of Arles was thought to have been martyred during the third or early fourth century: see Griffe (1964-1966) I:131, 144-5, and Vieillard-Troiekouroff (1976) 37-8. A sermon about his life is extant: ed. Cavallin (1945) 165-8 = *PL* Suppl.3.649-52; and, as Eusebius 'Gallicanus', *Homilia* LVI (50), ed. Fr.Glorie, *CChrL* 101A (1971) 651-4. An account of his martyrdom also survives: ed. *PL* 61.418-20, G.de Hartel, *CSEL* 29 (1894) 425-8, and Cavallin (1945) 160-4. Cavallin attributes the sermon to Hilarius, bishop of Arles from 430 until 449, and dates the account of the saint's martyrdom to the sixth century.

voice and said: "Blessed Genesius, save us by the power of your own holiness, lest the people who have faithfully and piously come to celebrate your festival perish." Soon a wind blew up and the entire crowd of people was brought to the bank. They marveled that they had been saved by the power of the martyr.[82]

Lombards and other enemies often broke the railing of his holy tomb. These men were possessed by a demon and seized by madness. They raged and bit themselves with their own teeth, but they carried off none of the objects they had violently taken.[83]

Some say that in Arles there was a woman whose husband accused her of a crime. Although the accusation was not proved at all, it was decided by a judge that she be submerged in the water. A huge stone was tied to her neck with ropes, and she was thrown from a boat into the Rhone river. But she begged for the assistance of the blessed martyr, invoked his name, and said: "St Genesius, glorious martyr, you who have sanctified these waters with the stroke of your swimming, rescue me because of my innocence!" Immediately she began to float on the waters. When the people saw this, they took her into the boat and brought her alive to the church of the saint. Neither her husband nor the judge investigated her further.

69. The woman accused of a misdeed.

Oh, how admirable is innocence, how deserving a pure mind! For in a similar situation another woman faced an accusation of adultery by her husband. For a long time she denied this accusation before a judge. Since she could not be convicted by her own confession, she was condemned to be submerged. The people rushed to this spectacle. The woman was led to a bridge over the Saône river, where a heavy stone was tied to her neck with a rope. As the people threw her into the river, her husband rebuked her from the bank and said: "With these

[82] According to the *Sermo de miraculo S. Genesii* (*PL* 50.1273-6), the saint rescued this broken pontoon bridge during the episcopacy of Honoratus from 427 until 430. This sermon has also been attributed with some probability to Hilarius, Honoratus' successor as bishop at Arles: see Griffe (1964-1966) III:224-6.

[83] Once the Lombards occupied northern Italy in 568 [*HF* IV.41], they and the Franks constantly fought and negotiated [*HF* IV.42, 44, V.20, VI.6, 24, 42, IX.20, 25, 29, X.3]: see Wickham (1981) 28-47.

abundant waters cleanse your fornications and your impurities with which you have often stained my bed." But the compassion of the Lord, which does not allow the innocent to perish, provided a stake beneath the waters that no one could see. This stake caught the rope and held the woman up, so that she did not fall to the bottom of the river. Both were beneath the waters, that is, the woman and the stone, balanced on the scale of the stake. When the sun was already setting, the relatives of the woman requested of the judge that they be allowed to search for the body of their kinswoman in the raging riverbed. Once permission was granted, they went to the spot where the woman had been thrown in. They saw her suspended with the stone, and by using a grappling hook they dragged her over. When they saw she was alive, they quickly brought her to the church that was next to the river, because they were afraid that the judge would order her to be submerged again. They asked the woman how she had been able to survive beneath the water. She replied: "To me it seemed no different than a dream. I never felt the waters except when I sank after being thrown in them and when I stood up after being rescued again from them." Everyone marveled that in such a dangerous situation she was not able to die. For the faith of her pure conscience and the Lord to whom she always prayed had saved her. Then she was restored to her parents, and neither the judge nor her husband investigated her further. But let us return to the miracles of the martyrs.[84]

70. The martyrs Ferreolus and Ferrucio.

Besançon is also distinguished by its own martyrs and often rejoices in current miracles. According to the account of their suffering, the two martyrs Ferreolus and Ferrucio were buried here in an obscure corner of a crypt. Once it happened that the husband of my sister was very ill with a high fever. Already he had lain gasping on his bed for

---

[84] An accusation of adultery was the most serious charge that could be brought against a woman, since it tainted her reputation and compromised the integrity of her family: see Wemple (1981) 41-3, and Rouche (1987) 471-3. The use of a judge and the ordeal of water may not have been common, because husbands and relatives might simply murder or burn adulteresses [*HF* VI.36, VIII.19]. In another case, after her adultery precipitated a bloody brawl between her father's and her husband's families, a woman committed suicide when summoned to appear before a court [*HF* V.32].

four months. Since his grieving wife could think of nothing else except what was required for his funeral, she wept and in her unhappiness went to the church of the saints. She knelt before their tombs, and she pressed her hands and face to the hard pavement. By chance it happened that the palm of her outstretched right hand closed on a leaf from the herb sage that had been scattered in the crypt in honor of the martyrs. Then, at the conclusion of her prayer, she rose in tears from the tombs. She thought she had taken in her hand something from the linen garments she was as usual wearing, and she kept her hand closed. After leaving the church, she opened her hand and was surprised by the leaf of the herb. Astounded at what it was, she recognized it as a gift from heaven granted to her by God, so that through it the power of the martyrs might no doubt assist her ill husband. She returned home in happiness, soaked the leaf in water, and offered the potion for her husband to drink. He was filled with faith, and when he drank the potion, immediately he was worthy to obtain his complete health.[85]

71. The martyr St Dionysius.

Bishop Dionysius was enrolled as a martyr at Paris. Once king Sigibert came with an army to Paris and destroyed many of its surrounding villages with a fire. One of his retainers hurried to the church of the aforementioned martyr, not out of devotion to offer a prayer but only so that he might steal something from the church. As soon as he discovered that the doors were unlocked and that no custodians were in the church, he rashly and boldly seized the silk shroud that was ornamented with gold and gems and that covered the holy tomb and took it off with himself. As he returned to the camp, it was necessary for him to take a boat. [With him] was his servant, whom he had always trusted and who had two hundred gold pieces hanging around his neck. When his servant boarded the boat with him, suddenly, although no one

[85] Ferreolus and Ferrucio were thought to have been martyred in the late second or early third century, although the evidence is dubious: see Griffe (1964-1966) I:143. The church containing their tombs was in Saint-Fergeux: see Vieillard-Troiekouroff (1976) 254-5. Gregory's sister (who is unnamed) had married Justinus, who also once received a cure from St Martin [*VM* 2.2]. Their daughter, named Justina, became prioress in the convent of Radegund at Poitiers and was threatened during the revolt there in 589 [*HF* X.15]: see Scheibelreiter (1979).

had touched him, he fell from the boat, was crushed by the waters, and could not be found again. The man recognized in the loss of the servant and the gold that God had passed judgement on himself. Quickly he returned to the shore from which he had departed, and with great haste he returned the shroud to the tomb. But even though he did this, he did not survive during the course of the coming year to the first anniversary of the day on which he had committed these crimes.

Another man was not afraid to step on the holy tomb while he wished to strike with his spear at the gold dove [attached to the tomb]. Because there was a tower on top of the tomb, the man's feet slipped on each side. He crushed his testicles, stabbed himself in the side with his spear, and was found dead. Let no one doubt that this happened not by chance, but by the judgement of God.[86]

72. The martyr Quintinus.

The martyr Quintinus is buried at the Gallic town of Saint-Quentin. A nun who had been blind for a long time found his holy body. As soon as the body was raised from the bottom of the river, it displayed a miracle; for at daybreak it restored to the eyes of the woman the sight that had been blinded.[87]

In this city a thief secretly stole a priest's horse. When the priest found him, he was brought to a judge. There was no delay: the thief was arrested, bound in chains, and handed over for torture. The thief revealed his deed with his own confession and was condemned to the gallows. But the priest feared lest on account of his accusation a man

---

[86] Gregory claimed that Dionysius had been one of the seven missionaries sent to Gaul in the middle of the third century and had been martyred at Paris [HF I.30]. Some members of the royal family were buried in the church dedicated to St Dionysius already in the sixth century [HF V.34]; by the seventh century the church and monastery at Saint-Denis had become the principal site for the tombs of members of the royal Merovingian family: see Vieillard-Troiekouroff (1976) 252-3, and Wallace-Hadrill (1983) 126-33, for royal patronage for the abbey of Saint-Denis. During a civil war between king Sigibert and his brother king Chilperic in 574 Sigibert's army pillaged Paris [HF IV.49]. On the day that the two kings finally concluded a treaty, three lame men were healed at the tomb of St Martin in Tours [VM 2.5-7].

[87] Quintinus was thought to have been martyred at the beginning of the fourth century, although the evidence is dubious: see Griffe (1964-1966) I:163, and Vieillard-Troiekouroff (1976) 272-3.

lose his life. So he begged the judge that he spare his life and that the
man accused of this crime be freed from this penalty. The priest said
that he was satisfied with what had already been done, because after so
many types of torture the thief had admitted what he had done. But no
prayers could bend the severity of the judge, and he condemned the
accused man to the gallows. Then the priest in tears bowed before the
tomb of the holy martyr and offered a prayer of supplication. He said:
"Most glorious athlete of Christ, I ask that you rescue this poor man
from the hand of an unjust death, so that I might not be ashamed if this
man dies as a result of my accusation. I beg you, display your power,
so that by the mitigation of your gentle piety you might release the
man whom human harshness could not forgive." After the priest wept
and offered this prayer, the chains on the gallows broke and the accused
man fell to the ground. When the judge heard of this, he was terrified
and marveled at this divine miracle; but he no longer dared to harm the
man.

73. The martyr Genesius of Tarbes.
   Within the territory of Tarbes there is another martyr [Genesius]
who held the rank of priest. The history of his suffering is read to the
inhabitants of the region. When Genesius was still alive, his prayers
made a chestnut tree that had been withered for a long time bloom
again. In his church miracles frequently are shown to ill people. But
this is thought to be the most remarkable miracle, that a lily, cut and
dried out long before, flowers again during his festival, so that on that
day people may admire how what they had previously seen to be
withered now blossoms anew. Often the power of the martyr disproves
the false oath that deceitful men had sworn at his tomb. A man who
comes elated by his rashness will hence leave after being corrected.[88]

74. King Sigismund.
   For the Lord often suppresses the arrogance of a stubborn mind
with his rod of correction so that he might restore the same mind to
respect for his worship. As clear confirmation there is the behavior of

---

[88] Genesius of Tarbes is otherwise unknown. Like Genesius of Thiers [GM
66], this Genesius may have been invented as a local double of Genesius of
Arles [GM 67-68]: see Griffe (1964-1966) I:140-1.

king Sigismund in the past. His heart was filled with remorse after he had killed his own son at the urging of his evil wife. He went to Saint-Maurice-d'Agaune, and there he knelt before the tombs of the most blessed martyrs of the propitious [Theban] Legion. He performed penance and prayed that divine vengeance would punish him for his misdeeds in this world, so that he might be considered absolved in judgement if he repaid the evils he had committed before he departed from the world. He instituted there the daily recitation of psalms, and he most generously enriched the place with new lands and with other endowments. Later he and his sons were captured by king Chlodomer, at whose order he was killed. His body was brought to the same place and buried in a tomb. This [following] event indicates that he was received into the company of the saints. For whenever people suffering from chills piously celebrate a mass in his honor and make an offering to God for the king's repose, immediately their tremors cease, their fevers disappear, and they are restored to their earlier health.[89]

75. The saints of Saint-Maurice-d'Agaune.

There is great power at the tombs of the aforementioned martyrs [of the Theban Legion]. Although many stories are omitted, it is appropriate to relate a few stories about these martyrs. A woman brought her only son to this monastery and gave him to the abbot for instruction, so that he might become a monk and be dedicated to the sacred ceremonies [of the liturgy]. But when he was already educated in the Bible and already chanted the psalms with the other monks in a chorus of

[89] For the Theban Legion and St Mauricius (or Maurice), see *GM* 61. Sigismund became a king of the Burgundians in 516. Although he had already accepted catholic Christianity, intra-familial murders characterized his reign. After he had his son by his first wife murdered in 522 because of the enmity of his second wife, he performed penance at the monastery of Saint-Maurice-d'Agaune that he had restored [*HF* III.5]. Queen Clotild, the widow of Clovis, then encouraged her sons to avenge the murder of her parents by Gundobad, Sigismund's father and her own uncle [*HF* II.28]. Chlodomer, one of her sons, captured Sigismund and his family and had them murdered in 523; the next year Chlodomer was killed in a battle against Sigismund's brother [*HF* III.6]: see Wood (1985) 253-4. In Gregory's perspective, Sigismund's subsequent "martyrdom" seems to have compensated for the murder of his own son. A *Passio* of Sigismund survives, composed probably in the early eighth century: ed. B.Krusch, *MGH*, SRM 2 (1888) 333-40.

singers, he was struck by a slight fever and died. His mother was bereaved; she wept at the ritual of his funeral and buried her son. But the tears shed at his funeral were not adequate for her grief. Every day she came, and directing her cries to heaven she mourned over the tomb of her son. Finally one night the blessed Mauricius appeared to her in a vision and asked: "O woman, why do you incessantly mourn the death of your son? Are you never to cease from your grief?" She replied to him: "The days of my life are not sufficient for this grief, but so long as I am alive I will always weep for my only son. Tears will never sooth me, until the death that is my destiny closes the eyes of my body." Mauricius said to her: "Do not mourn as if your son is dead; instead, compose yourself. Know that he is living with us and is enjoying the habitation of eternal life in our company. And so that you may believe with more certainty that I speak the truth, rise for matins tomorrow. You will hear his voice among the chorus of monks who are chanting the psalms. And not only tomorrow but also every day of your life when you attend you will hear his voice in the chanting of psalms. Do not weep, because it is proper that you rejoice rather than grieve." The woman arose and sighed at length. In her own bed she did not sleep until the monks sounded the bell for rising. When the bell was rung, she went to the church to verify something in the vision that she had seen. For nothing from the saint's promise was missing, and what had been announced by God was soon known to have been fulfilled. After the singing of the response the mother listened when the choir of monks chanted the antiphon. She heard the voice of her young son, and she gave thanks to God. And that [other] promise which had been pledged by the mouth of the martyr was also immediately fulfilled. Thereafter, during all the days of her life whenever the woman attended the chanting of psalms, she heard the voice of her young son among the melodies of others' voices.

King Guntramn so dedicated himself to spiritual behavior that he abandoned the trappings of this world and spent his wealth on churches and the poor. It happened that, in accordance with his vow, he sent a priest to bring gifts to the brothers who served the saints at Saint-Maurice-d'Agaune. He ordered the priest to bring him relics of the saints upon his return. Then, after the priest fulfilled the king's command, while he was returning with these relics, he sought a boat at Lake Leman, through which the Rhone river flows. This lake is about four hundred stades long and one hundred and fifty stades wide. While the priest was returning, as I said, he boarded this boat. Suddenly a storm arose and whipped up the waves. Waves as high as mountains rose to the stars. When the prow sank, the stern of the ship was tossed in the air; when the stern was submerged, in turn the prow was tossed in the air. The sailors were frantic and in such danger wished only for death. The priest then saw that they were being overpowered by these waves and buried beneath the violent foam of the waves. He took from his neck the reliquary that held the relics of the saints and in his faith threw it into the swelling waves. With a loud voice he invoked the protection of the saints and said: "Glorious martyrs, I request your power so that I may not die in these waves. I ask that you who always offer assistance to those who are dying instead deign to extend your right hand of salvation to me. Calm the waves, and with the strength of your assistance lead us to the shore we hope for." As he said this, the wind died down, the waves subsided, and they were brought to shore. I heard this story from the priest himself. For some say that in Lake Leman the size of the trout reaches even the weight of one hundred [Roman] pounds.[90]

76. Victor of Marseilles.

At the tomb of St Victor, a martyr of Marseilles, there is marvelous power. For not only are ill people often healed after approaching his tomb, but the other possessed people, who are often bruising themselves and shouting out the martyr's name, are freed after their demons have been expelled. The servant of the patrician Aurilianus was possessed by a demon and suffered from a terrible calamity, with the result that often he bit himself with his own teeth. He was brought to the church of the saint. After he announced that he was burning because of the saint's power, he danced through the entire church. Three

---

[90] Although the monastery at Saint-Maurice-d'Agaune was apparently already in existence at the beginning of the sixth century, the patronage of king Sigismund helped it become an important monastic center: see Masai (1971), Vieillard-Troiekouroff (1976) 265-8, and Wood (1981) 15-17. King Guntramn reigned from 561 until 593. According to Gregory, Lake Leman was almost fifty miles long and twenty miles wide and thus larger than it is today: see Weidemann (1982) II:341. The trout he mentioned would weigh about seventy-two English pounds—heavy enough to suspect that Gregory has here swallowed someone's fish story!

days later he was cleansed and left. He was so strengthened in the reward of his faith that he was tonsured, achieved the rank of abbot, and presided over a monastery.[91]

77. The martyr St Baudilius.

The glorious tomb of the blessed martyr Baudilius is in Nîmes. Many miracles are revealed at his tomb. A laurel grows from his tomb. Sticking out through a wall, it becomes a tree outside with lush and beneficial foliage. The inhabitants of the region realized that this tomb often possessed a heavenly remedy for many illnesses. Since the tree had been repeatedly stripped of its leaves and some of its bark to obtain the benefits of its powers, it had become withered. Although I noted that the diseases of many ill people were cured by this tree, it would take a long time to list each individually. Therefore I have thought that this was adequate [proof], because I mentioned that the tree had become withered by dispensing these medicines. It is frequently said that a merchant brought a relic of these leaves to the East. Even before the merchant put into port, a possessed man announced in a church to the surprised congregation that the martyr Baudilius was arriving in the eastern regions.

The blessed martyr revealed his power also in other circumstances. While Ara, a duke of king Theodoric of Italy, was residing in Arles, there was an archpriest from a parish of Nîmes whom he hated. The duke burned with animosity and sent soldiers against him. He said: "Go as quickly as possible. Bind his hands and feet and forcibly bring him, so that he may know that I am the master of this region." The young men misunderstood [his order about the] archpriest and thought he was ordering the archdeacon to be brought to him. They mounted their horses, came to the city, and asked about the archdeacon, who was pointed out to them. This archdeacon was named Johannes. He was a truly pious man and as archdeacon had the task of teaching young boys. The duke's soldiers seized him, bound his hands and feet beneath the

---

[91] Victor (or Victorius) was a prominent citizen of Marseille thought to have been martyred at the end of the third century: see Griffe (1964-1966) I:154-5. The patrician Aurilianus is perhaps to be identified with Aurelianus, the praetorian prefect in Gaul in 473: see Stroheker (1948) no.46, Mathisen (1982) 367, and Heinzelmann (1982) 564.

belly of a horse, and brought him [to Arles]. But the power of the
martyr was not lacking to assist his own foster son. The soldiers
encamped with him next to the gate; they could not enter because the
doors of the gates had been closed for the night. But during the night
the archdeacon appeared in a vision to the duke while he was asleep and
said: "O man, why did you think I was guilty, so that you have ordered
me to be treated so shamefully and to be summoned with such dis-
regard? But let me say to you that you will not escape the judgement
of God." The duke awoke and was petrified with fear, and he said to his
servants: "Find out whether the soldiers whom I sent to Nîmes have
already returned." After they asked from the wall of the city, the
soldiers replied that they were there with the man. The messengers
reported what they had heard. Immediately the duke said: "Show me
the man whom you have brought." When they did so, the duke looked
at him, was terrified, and said: "I ordered that the archpriest, not the
archdeacon, be brought." The duke knelt at the archdeacon's feet and
said: "I beg you, forgive this wrong deed, because it was not my
intention that you suffer these indignities." And immediately he
honored the archdeacon with appropriate gifts and sent him back to
Nîmes. Because of his reverence for the martyr, the duke thereafter
cherished the city with such love that, when its bishop died, he ordered
that this archdeacon be ordained as bishop. But he never again ordered
the archpriest to be sought out. O great power of the martyr that
absolves from a penalty a man guilty of wronging an innocent man!
The saying of the apostle was fulfilled: "For those who love God all
things work together for good" [Romans 8:28]. For this insult formed
a step for this archdeacon that he climbed to governance in the church of
God.[92]

78. The cathedral at Agde.
    The cathedral at Agde, which rejoices in its relics of the apostle St
Andrew, often is distinguished by glorious miracles and often exposes
those who invade its possessions. Count Gomacharius invaded a field

[92] Nothing certain is known about Baudilius (or Baudillius): see Griffe
(1964-1966) I:144-6, and Vieillard-Troiekouroff (1976) 194-5. Ara was duke at
Arles sometime between 510 and 526, when king Theodoric of the Ostrogoths
died: see Heinzelmann (1982) 557.

belonging to this cathedral. Leo, the bishop of this cathedral, was very upset and rushed to the count; he said: "O my son, depart from the possessions of the poor that the Lord has entrusted to my rule, lest it be harmful to you and lest you die from the tears of the needy who are accustomed to eat the produce of this field." But the count, because he was a heretic, disregarded what the bishop said and kept the field under his own control. As the day went on, he was struck with a fever. Since he suffered not only from his bodily fever but also from torment in his heart, he sent messengers to the bishop and said: "Let the bishop deign to offer a prayer on my behalf to the Lord, and I will forsake his field." After the bishop prayed, the count recovered from the illness that afflicted him. After regaining his health, he said to his servants: "What do you think these Romans are now saying? They say that I was afflicted with this fever because I had seized their field. But the fever affected me according to the nature of the human body; and since I am still alive they will not have the field." After saying this, he quickly sent a man who again seized the field. When the bishop learned of this, he went to the count and said: "Do you already regret to have done a good deed, so that you attempt again to do the opposite? I ask you, do not do this, and do not expose yourself to divine vengeance." The count said to the bishop: "Be quiet, be quiet, you decrepit man. I will have you bound with the reins to ride around the city on an ass, so that everyone who sees you might ridicule you." The bishop was silent and returned to his familiar protection [in the cathedral]. He knelt in prayer, kept vigils, and spent the entire night weeping and chanting psalms. At daybreak he went to the lamps that hung from the rafters of the cathedral, stretched out the staff that he held in his hand, and broke all the lights. He said: "No light will be lit here until God takes vengeance on his enemies and restores this field that belongs to his house." As he said this, immediately the heretic collapsed from a revived fever. When he was on the verge of death, he sent to the bishop and said: "Let the bishop pray to the Lord for me, so that I might live and restore the field and grant another similar field to his control." The bishop replied to his words: "I have already prayed to the Lord, and he has heard me." The count sent a second embassy to him, and then a third. But the bishop persisted in his one response and was not influenced to pray to the Lord for the count. When the heretic realized this, he ordered that he be placed on a wagon and brought to the bishop to beg him in person. He said: "I will restore with double restitution the field that I have unjustly taken, so that your holiness might pray for me." When the bishop refused, the count forcibly compelled him to go to the cathedral. As the bishop left to enter the cathedral, the count died. Immediately the church took back its property.[93]

79. The wickedness of a heretic.

Heresy is always hostile to catholics, and wherever it can set snares it does not pass over [the opportunity]. An example is this story that rumor widely claims happened in a certain place. There was a catholic woman who had a heretical husband. When a catholic priest of our religion visited her, the woman said to her husband: "I ask of your charity that at the arrival of this priest who has deigned to visit me there might be a celebration in our house, and that we might share with him a meal prepared with the appropriate expense." Her husband agreed to do what she had asked. Then a priest of the heretics arrived, and the man said to his wife: "Today our celebration is doubled, because priests of both religions are in our house." As they sat down for the meal, the husband sat at the head [of the table] with the [heretical] priest on his right hand and put the catholic priest on his left hand. His wife sat on a stool placed at his left. The husband said to the heretical priest: "If you agree with my words, let us today mock this priest of the Romans. When the food is brought out, you hurry to bless it first. Since he will grieve and not place his hand on it, we will happily eat the food." The heretical priest replied: "I will do what you command." When the platter with the vegetables arrived, the heretical priest blessed it and was the first to put his hand on it. The woman saw this and said: "Do not do that, because I am unwilling for the catholic priest to be insulted." When other food was brought, the catholic priest took some. But the heretical priest performed the same [blessing] over the second and third courses. The fourth course was brought out, in the middle of which

---

[93] Leo was bishop at Agde at some time between 506 and c.567: see Duchesne (1894-1915) I:306, and Weidemann (1982) I:135. Since Gregory described Gomacharius as a heretic, he presumably was a count appointed by the Arian Visigoths in Spain. In the early 580s Agde was still under Visigothic control [*HF* VI.2]; shortly after 579 the Visigothic king Leovigild drove Phronimius, the catholic bishop of Agde, into exile [*HF* IX.24]: see Thompson (1969) 81-2.

was a hot pan in which the food lay. The food consisted of whipped eggs mixed with a little flour and was garnished as usual with chopped dates and round olives. Before the food had even touched the table, the heretical priest lifted his hand in the way and hurried to bless it. He immediately put out his spoon and took a portion. Not knowing whether it was hot, he quickly swallowed the fiery food. Suddenly his throat was on fire and he began to burn. His stomach rumbled, he belched loudly, and he exhaled his worthless spirit. After he was taken from the feast, he was put in a tomb and covered with a pile of dirt. The priest of our religion was happy and said: "Truly God has avenged his servants." He turned to the husband who was hosting the dinner and said: "The memory of this man has perished with the sound he made, and the Lord remains in eternity. But bring something for me to eat." The husband was frightened, and after the meal he knelt at the feet of the priest and converted to the catholic faith. Along with his entire household, which this treachery had gripped, he believed. And just as his wife had requested, the celebration was multiplied.

80. The argument between a catholic deacon and a heretical priest.

An Arian priest had an argument with a deacon of our religion. As is customary with his kind, he made poisonous assertions against the Son of God and the Holy Spirit. Often the deacon offered at length some arguments about the logic of our faith, but the heretic was blinded by the darkness of his treachery and rejected what was true, in accordance with that saying: "Wisdom will not enter an evil soul" [Wisdom of Solomon 1:4] So the deacon added to his comments and said: "Why do we wear ourselves out with the long exertions of words? The truth of a thing is determined by deeds. Let a bronze pot be heated over a fire, and let someone's ring be thrown into the boiling water. Whoever recovers the ring from the boiling water will be proven to follow righteousness. Once this is done, the other side will be converted to recognition of this righteousness. Understand, heretic, that with the assistance of the Holy Spirit our side will perform the task. You will confess that in the holy Trinity there is nothing discordant and nothing dissimilar." The heretic agreed to these rules, and they left after agreeing that the trial would begin in the morning. But because the enemy was setting an ambush, the fervent faith through which the deacon had first made his proposal began to cool down. Rising at dawn, he spread salve on his arm and sprinkled it with an ointment. He walked around the holy shrines and prayed to the Lord. Why say more? About the third hour they met in a public place. The people gathered for the spectacle. A fire was lit, the bronze pot was hung over it and became very hot, and a ring was thrown into the boiling water. The deacon first invited the heretic to recover the ring from the heat. But he immediately refused and said: "You who proposed the idea ought to recover it." Although afraid, the deacon bared his arm. When the heretical priest saw that his arm was covered with ointments, he cried out and said: "You thought that you must be protected by magical skills, so you smeared these ointments [on your arm]. But what you do will not help you." While these two were arguing, Jacincthus, a deacon from Ravenna, came and asked what the argument was about. When he learned the truth, he did not delay. He exposed his arm from his sleeve and plunged his right hand into the bronze pot. The ring that had been thrown in was very light and small, and it was tossed about by the water no less than chaff can be tossed up by the wind. After searching for a long time the man found the ring in the space of one hour. Meanwhile the fire was burning fiercely beneath the pot; the ring was hence very hot, and the hand of the man looking for it could not easily touch it. After the deacon had retrieved the ring, he felt nothing on his flesh. Instead, he insisted that the bronze pot was cold at the bottom and slightly warm at the top. When the heretic heard this, he was very upset and boldly plunged his own hand into the bronze pot. He said: "My faith will produce the same results for me." As soon as he put his hand in the water, immediately his flesh was melted down to the very joints of his bones and fell off. So the argument ended.

81. The cleric who was tortured for confessing the Lord.

The disbelief and the wicked sect of the Arians had spread into the regions of Spain by means of harmful assertions of evil. During our time a cleric was captured. He confessed that he was a Christian and claimed that the Son and the Holy Spirit were equal to the Father. The king who then ruled offered gifts to the cleric and humbly begged him, as if begging a superior, to recant his confession about the equality of the holy Trinity and say that the Son and the Holy Spirit were inferior to the Father. If the cleric did this, he would be enriched with possessions and would be considered a great man among the people. When the cleric avoided this advice as if it were a viper's bite and rejected the deathbearing poison of this evil snake, the king added: "I see the hard determination of an insane mind, but I know your personality, so that tortures will easily undermine you whom gifts cannot bend." The cleric said: "If only I might be worthy to be killed for this confession, because I reject your gifts as if [they were] manure." Then the king was angry. He ordered the cleric to be stretched on the rack and cruelly tortured. He asked: "What do you believe?" The cleric replied: "I have already told you. I believe in God the omnipotent Father and his Son Jesus Christ." Then the cleric was terribly tortured, but always he persisted in his confession; these tortures could not deflect him from the straight line of his faith. For when he was first being tortured, he felt only three blows from the lashes that penetrated his soul, as he later always claimed. As if some covering had been placed over his back, he never felt the other lashes; instead, while enduring such torments he displayed more faith than he had initially. When the king was satisfied with his torture, the cleric was released; the king warned that he never be found again within the boundaries of Spain.[94] The cleric happily left and returned to Gaul. So that these words might be considered reliable, I saw a man who told this story that he had heard from the mouth of the cleric himself.

82. The power of the relics that were brought to me from Rome.

Through their confession the glorious martyrs have earned the unspeakable benefits of gifts that are always salutary. To petitioners they have revealed themselves by this power that the Lord Creator shared with them. I know that this happened just as my deacon recently told me. This deacon received relics of some martyrs and confessors from pope Pelagius of Rome. A large chorus of monks who were chanting psalms and a huge crowd of people escorted him to Ostia. After he boarded a ship the sails were unfurled and hoisted over the rigging of a mast that presented the appearance of a cross. As the wind

[94] This incident of torture probably happened during the reign of Leovigild, who was sole king of the Visigoths from 571 or 573 until 586 [*HF* IV.38, VIII.46]. By proposing a modified form of Arian theology about the status of the members of the Trinity he attempted to promote a centralized autocratic kingship in his realm; but in the early 580s civil war broke out with his son Hermenegild, who eventually converted to catholic Christianity: see Thompson (1969) 57-91, and the revised interpretation of Collins (1980) and (1983) 45-9.

blew, they set out on the high seas. While they were sailing to reach the port of Marseilles, they began to approach a certain place where a mountain of stone rose from the shore of the sea and, sinking a bit, stretched into the sea to the top of the water. As the wind forced them on, the ship was lifted by a mighty blast into danger. When the ship was shaken as if struck by the rock, the sailors recognized their peril and announced their death. The deacon lifted the reliquary with the holy relics. He groaned and in a loud voice began to invoke the names of the individual saints. He prayed that their power might liberate from danger those who were about to die. The ship, as I said, sailed closer and closer to the rock. Suddenly, out of respect for the holy relics, a wind blew from that spot with great force against the other wind. It crushed the waves and repulsed the opposing wind. By recalling the ship to the deep sea, the wind freed everyone from the danger of death. So they circumvented this impending danger, and by the grace of the Lord and the protection of the saints they arrived at the port they had hoped for. For these were relics of the saints whose sacred feet had been washed by the hands of the Lord. [There were also relics] of Paul, Laurentius, Pancratius, Chrysanthus, the virgin Daria, and John and his brother, the other Paul. Rome, the capital of the world, piously celebrates their struggles and the prizes of their victories.[95]

83. The relics that my father owned.

I will now narrate what happened with regard to the relics that my father once carried with him. At the time when Theudebert ordered the sons of Clermont to be sent off as hostages, my father had been recently married. Because he wished himself to be protected by relics of

---

[95] This deacon may well have been Agiulf, who was in Rome for the consecration of pope Gregory I in 590 after the death of Pelagius II [*HF* X.1] and who also stopped in Lyon on his return [*VP* 8.6]. If this identification is correct, then Gregory wrote at least this chapter of the *GM* during the early 590s. In contrast, O.Chadwick (1948), argues that Gregory's deacon was in fact in Rome during the 580s: but see Krusch (1951) xx n.3, and Buchner (1955) xxv n.1. Gregory had already mentioned some of these saints from Rome, including Paul [*GM* 28], Laurentius [*GM* 41, 45], Pancratius [*GM* 38], and Chrysanthus and Daria [*GM* 37]. John and the other Paul were brothers and eunuchs who were thought to have been martyred at Rome during the reign of the emperor Julian from 361 to 363: see C.Pietri (1976) 484-5.

saints, he asked a cleric to grant him something from these relics, so that with their protection he might be kept safe as he set out on this long journey. He put the sacred ashes in a gold medallion and carried it with him. Although he did not even know the names of the blessed men, he was accustomed to recount that he had been rescued from many dangers. He claimed that often, because of the powers of these relics, he had avoided the violence of bandits, the dangers of floods, the threats of turbulent men, and attacks from swords.[96]

I will not be silent about what I witnessed regarding these relics. After the death of my father my mother carried these relics with her. It was the time for harvesting the crops, and huge piles of grain had been collected on the threshing floors. Just like the Limagne, which is clothed with crops but stripped of its trees,[97] so during those days when the seeds were already threshed there was no place to light a fire when a frost appeared. So the threshers kindled fires for themselves from the straw. Then everyone retired to eat. And behold, the fire gradually began to be spread through the straw bit by bit. Quickly, fanned by the wind, the fire spread to the piles of grain. The fire became a huge blaze and was accompanied by the shouts of men, the wails of women, and the crying of children. This happened in our field. When my mother, who was wearing these relics around her neck, learned of this, she rushed from the meal and held the sacred relics in front of the balls of flames. In a moment the entire fire so died down that no sparks were

---

[96] When Theudebert heard that his father king Theuderic was dying in 533, he left his family at Clermont [*HF* III.23]. Since Florentius, Gregory's father, belonged to a locally prominent family that claimed "senatorial" status [*VP* 14.3], he may have been one of the hostages held to guarantee the safety of Theudebert's family. Florentius seems to have been a generation older than Armentaria, Gregory's mother; their surviving children included Gregory, born in 538 or 539, his older brother Peter [*VJ* 24], and a sister [cf. *GM* 70]. Gregory elsewhere recorded a story he had heard from his father [*VP* 14.3], and mentioned how, when he was still a young boy, he had helped cure his father's gout [*GC* 39]. Florentius died when Gregory was still young, and Armentaria eventually went to live in Chalon-sur-Saône, in her family's native region of Burgundy [*VM* 3.60, *GC* 3, 84]. By then Gregory was a young man and had acquired his father's reliquary.

[97] The Limagne is a plain in the southern Auvergne and was noted for its fertility and beauty [*HF* III.9, V.33].

found among the piles of burned straw and the seeds. The grain the fire had touched had suffered no harm.

Many years later I received these relics from my mother. While I was travelling from Burgundy to Clermont, a huge storm appeared in my path. The storm frequently flashed with lightning in the sky and rumbled with loud crashes of thunder. Then I took the holy relics from my pocket and raised my hand before the cloud. The cloud immediately divided into two parts and passed by on the right and the left; it threatened neither me nor anyone else. Then, as a presumptuous young man is expected to behave, I began to be inflated by the arrogance of vain glory. I silently thought that this concession had been made especially for me, rather than because of the merits of the saints. I boasted to my travelling companions and insisted that I had deserved that which God had bestowed upon my naïveté. Immediately my horse suddenly slipped beneath me and threw me to the ground. I was so seriously bruised during this accident that I could hardly get up. I understood that this accident had happened because of my pride; and it was sufficient to note that afterwards the urge of vain glory did not bother me. For if it happened that I was worthy to observe some manifestations of the powers of saints, I have proclaimed that they were due to the gift of God through the faith of the saints.

84. The man who washed his feet in a paten belonging to a church.

Rashness is totally without benefit, with the result that someone desires what it is not permissible to do. A count of Brittany suffered severely from pains in his feet and spent his fortune on doctors. When he had no relief, one of his servants said to him: "If one of the liturgical vessels that are on the altar would be brought to you from the church, and if you washed your feet in it, this could offer you a cure from your affliction." These were silly and idle men who did not know that the sacred vessels of God should not be adapted to human use. But the count quickly sent [men] to the church, took from the sacristy a silver paten [used] on the holy altar, and washed his feet in it. Immediately he suffered additional pains and was totally crippled; thereafter he was unable to walk. I have learned that a duke of the Lombards did the same thing.

85. The deacon whose hands a tower-shaped vessel avoided.

We weep and mourn for our crimes, since we do not know [whether] we are pure as we approach the altar of the Lord. Although we are polluted in the act, we boldly receive his holy body and blood as a judgement rather than so that we might obtain forgiveness [cf. I Corinthians 11:27-32]. For I recall what I heard happened when I was a young man. It was the anniversary of the suffering of the great martyr Polycarp, and a mass was being celebrated in Riom, a village in the territory of Clermont. [An account of] Polycarp's suffering was read along with the other readings that the clerical canon included. It was time for offering the sacrifice. A deacon took the tower-shaped vessel that held the mystery of the Lord's body [i.e. the unconsecrated bread] and began to bring it to the door. He entered the church to place the vessel on the altar. But the vessel floated above his hand and was carried by the air. As he advanced to the altar, the deacon's hand could never grip the vessel. I believe that this happened for no other reason than because he was polluted in his conscience. For some say that he often committed adultery. Only one priest and three women, among them my mother, were permitted to see this; the others did not see it. I confess, I was present then at the festival, but I was not worthy to see this.[98]

86. The priest who drank [wine] during a vigil on Christmas Eve.

So also when the priest Epachius rashly presumed to do what he was unworthy of, he was struck by divine judgement and fell to the ground. For after he had entered the church to celebrate the vigils of Christmas Eve, for parts of each hour he left the church of God and in his own house lustfully swallowed some drinks from foaming cups. Many claimed to have seen him drinking during that night after cock-crow. But since he was a member of a senatorial family and since in the aforementioned village of Riom no one was more noble according to the ranking of this world, he was expected to celebrate the ceremony of mass. The wretched man, already drunk with wine, did not hesitate to do what someone who was fasting could not do without feeling fear and having a frightened conscience. After reciting the sacred words and

[98] The traditional date for the martyrdom of bishop Polycarp of Smyrna is c.155.

breaking the sacrament of the Lord's body, Epachius took [the bread] and distributed it for others to eat. Soon, whinnying like a horse, he fell to the ground. He foamed at the mouth and spat out the crumb of the holy mystery that he could not break with his teeth. His servants carried him from the church in their hands. Nor was he thereafter free from attacks of this epilepsy. Each month he suffered at the waxing and waning of the moon, because the wretch never abstained from drinking too much wine.[99]

This following example indicates with what respect and with what reverence Christmas Eve ought to be celebrated. Once when I had left the vigil of this festival, I was napping a bit. A man came to me and said: "Get up and return to the cathedral [of Tours]." I awoke, made the sign of the cross as protection [against the man], and went back to sleep. The same thing happened, and the same man repeated his earlier words. Although warned a second time, I did not get up, but again went to sleep. The man approached a third time and slapped my jaw. He said: "Behold, you ought to warn others to [attend] vigils; but are you still overcome by sleep?" Then I was thoroughly frightened and I swiftly ran back to the cathedral. This will suffice with regard to the vigil of Christmas Eve. But let us return to rash people.

87. The adulterous woman at the Jordan river.

An adulterous woman at Jericho had a most disgusting habit. Whenever she gave birth to a child conceived from prostitution, immediately she suffocated the child and buried it in the ground, so that what was not concealed from God and his angels would be hidden to men. When the holy day of Epiphany came, everyone went to the Jordan river to cleanse the sores of their bodies and the scars on their hearts. This woman went with the other people to the bank of the river. She lifted her garments to her knees to enter the river. But, amazing to say so, the water receded in front of her feet. When the woman followed the

[99] This Epachius was probably Eparchius, son of bishop Ruricius of Limoges and a priest at Clermont at the end of the fifth century whose family also included a former emperor and a former bishop of Clermont: see Mathisen (1982) 371, Heinzelmann (1982) 596, and Wood (1983) 37. In early Merovingian Gaul other families also still claimed "senatorial" status, sometimes with less warrent: see Gilliard (1979), and Brennan (1985b).

water, the river pressed up against the opposite bank. The people saw this and were surprised that such a thing happened on this illustrious day. Once they found out that this woman was the culprit, they asked what crime she had committed so that in this crowd of people this had happened [only] to her. The woman turned to the people, confessed her crime, and said: "Already I have murdered seven children born to me whom I conceived in immorality and feared to acknowledge. Yesterday I struck [and killed] my eighth child. So I ask that you pray for me to the Lord that my wickedness be forgiven and I cease to sin, so that the celestial anger does not consume me." After she spoke, all the people knelt on the ground and prayed to the Lord that in his mercy he forgive this woman for what she had done under the influence of weakness. After the prayer the woman stretched her arms out over the ground and died. I think that this happened so that the crime that had been pardoned could never be repeated. But the people now knew the misdeed and why the waters of the river had receded from the face of the woman. The proverb of Solomon was fulfilled: "The Spirit of the Lord flees from deceit" [Wisdom of Solomon 1:5]. I learned about this miracle from the mouth of the deacon Johannes. He claimed that he had been present at the time.[100]

88. The tomb of an unworthy man.

At Toulouse some say there was a man named Antoninus who was an enemy of God and the most hateful of all men because he had committed many crimes. It happened that after completing the days [of his life] he migrated from this world. He was buried in the church of the blessed Vincentius, in which while alive he had prepared a tomb. One night, while drowsiness seized everyone in a deep silence and everyone quietly rested their limbs in soothing sleep, that man's sarcophagus was thrown out of the holy church through a window and dumped in the middle of the courtyard. At daybreak it was found there, with its lid cracked. The man's relatives did not understand the power of God and did not realize the insult suffered by the saint in whose church they had rashly buried this unworthy man. They placed the sarcophagus

---

[100] This story seems out of place, since Gregory had included other stories about the Jordan river and Jericho much earlier [*GM* 16-20], among them one that he had learned about from Johannes [*GM* 18].

in the same place as previously and buried it deeper. But at the next daybreak they found it again thrown outside in the middle of the court-yard. Then they understood the great deeds of God. Thereafter no one touched the sarcophagus, and still today it remains as a witness in the place where it was thrown. Let these stories about rash people suffice.[101]

89. The deacon and martyr Vincentius.

Vincentius, both a deacon and a martyr, consummated his martyr-dom in Spain. Within the territory of Poitiers, in Herbauge, is the village of Bessay, which has relics of Vincentius. His festival is cele-brated on the twelfth day of the Kalends of the eleventh month [i.e. January; so the date is December 21]. But the inhabitants of the village and even their archpriest made some sort of mistake and wished to cele-brate it a day early. After celebrating mass they sat down at a feast. But one of the possessed people began to shout and said: "Hurry up, citizens, leave the village, go to meet the blessed Vincentius! Behold, he comes for his vigils! Behold, you will celebrate his festival tomorrow!" Once he said this, they started the rituals again and spent the entire night in vigils. While they were celebrating the mysteries of mass at daybreak, the possessed man who had announced the arrival of the saint and two others in addition were cured. Two paralytics were also healed on that day. And so the festival ended with great happiness.

When some travellers were transporting relics of Vincentius, they came to Céré, a village [in the territory] of Tours. They brought the relics to the cottage of a poor man, where they received lodging. On the next day two paralytics recovered their mobility in the presence of these relics and one blind man received his sight.

Not far from this village is another village called Orbigny, whose church has relics of this saint. Thieves stole these relics. The man who stole the relics left them with an abbot in Bourges, after being paid. The abbot had a vision that he should restore the relics to the place from which they had been removed. Likewise an archpriest who was a neighbor of the monastery had a vision that he should contrive no delays for the restoration [of the relics]. He received the relics and, to

---

[101] The identification of this church dedicated to St Vincentius [*GM* 89] is uncertain: see Vieillard-Troiekouroff (1976) 300.

the chanting of psalms, transported them [to Orbigny]. A man who suffered from a serious illness and had been laid up for an entire year was carried by the hands of his servants so that he might honor the shroud that covered the holy ashes. As a suppliant he kissed the shroud. His illness soon vanished and he was healed. Along with the other people he followed the procession of the martyr.[102]

90. The virgin and martyr Eulalia.

The glorious Eulalia suffered at Merida. On the anniversary of her sacrifice she demonstrates a great miracle to the people. In front of the altar that covers her sacred limbs there are three trees, although I do not know what kind they are. When her suffering is celebrated in the middle of the tenth month [December], the trees are stripped of any ornamenting foliage. But as the sky brightens on her festival day, the trees produce sweet blossoms in the shape of a swift dove; for her blessed spirit entered heaven in the shape of a dove and snow falling from heaven covered her blessed body, when it was already lifeless and stripped of its garments, with soft wool. If the trees produce this miracle with the usual spontaneity, the people know that their year will be free from problems and filled with crops. But if flowers bloom more slowly than usual, the people know that this threatens their own affairs. For already before the trees bloom the people bring their grievances and

[102] Vincentius was thought to have been martyred in the early fourth century. King Childebert and king Chlothar had invaded Spain in c.541 and besieged Saragossa; but they left when they heard about the power of the tunic of St Vincentius [HF III.29]. Childebert must have brought back relics of the saint, since he built a church in his honor at Paris in which he was himself buried in 558 [HF IV.20] and bishop Germanus of Paris in 576 [HF V.8, GC 88]: see Vieillard-Troiekouroff (1976) 211-4. Wandering holy men also claimed to have relics of St Vincentius [HF IX.6]: see de Lacger (1927), and Rouche (1979) 312-13, for his subsequent cult. The people at Bessay were only wrong by a day in celebrating the festival of St Vincentius; but unless there is a mistake in the manuscripts or Gregory was using a different system of numbering the months, the date he gave was apparently wrong by a month: see Waitz apud Krusch (1885) 547 n.7, and des Graviers (1946) 105. Eufronius, bishop of Tours from 556 until 573, built a church dedicated to St Vincentius in Tours [HF X.31] and perhaps also this one at Orbigny [cf. GM 30]; men transporting the relics to these new churches may have stopped at Céré: see Vieillard-Troiekouroff (1976) 77, 195-6, 326, and L.Pietri (1983) 497-8.

their quarrels to the tomb of the martyr and pray that they might be worthy to see the usual favor. If the blossoms have not appeared, there is no procession or chanting of psalms. But if the martyr is placated by the tears of the people, immediately flowers resembling gem stones blossom on the trees. The flowers emit the fragrance of nectar, and they make the sadness of the heart happy with their appearance and refresh it with their sweetness. Then the blossoms are carefully collected and brought to the bishop in the church. A procession joyously celebrates [them]. I know that these blossoms often assist ill people.[103]

91. The martyr Felix of Gerona.

Once thieves broke into the church of the martyr Felix. This martyr suffered in Gerona, a city in Spain. One thief seized the silk shrouds that were woven with gold [threads] and ornamented with jewels and took them with the other decorations. As he was leaving, a stranger met him and asked where he was going. The thief replied to him: "If you will keep my words secret, I will show you a huge treasure." The stranger replied: "Show me what you wish; with all my strength I will conceal it." The thief showed him some jewels and said: "If these valuables are sold in other regions, they will bring a great profit to both of us." The stranger said: "I am a man who has many friends in various regions, and my house is huge and secluded. If you store your valuables in it, you may sell them whenever is convenient." The stranger set out and the thief followed with his pack, thinking that he was being led to another city. For God closed his eyes, and he did not realize that he was returning on the road on which he had come. Why say more? Once they arrived at the church of the saint, the stranger said: "Behold the house which I mentioned to you! Enter and set your pack down!" The thief entered. But after he put down his pack, he began to look around and came to his senses. He recognized the church of the saint from which he had stolen the valuables. But the stranger had already left him. So the thief told the people everything he

---

[103] Eulalia was thought to have been martyred in the early fourth century. For the details of the dove and the snow Gregory perhaps used the account of her gruesome martyrdom in Prudentius, *Peristephanon* 3, ed. and trans. H.J.Thomson, LCL (1949-1953) II:142-57.

had done with that man. As a result, there is no doubt that the blessed
martyr himself had appeared to him.

A church at Narbonne has relics of Felix. But since the height of
this building prevented the very beautiful plain of the Livière from
being seen from the palace of king Alaric, he discussed the matter with
his adviser Leo. Leo said: "Let a section of the rafters be removed
from this building; then the king will more easily see what has pleased
him." The adviser Leo quickly summoned workmen and lowered the
church of the saint to [the height of] ordinary buildings. But Leo
immediately lost the sight of his eyes.[104]

92. The martyrs Emeterius and Chelidonius.

Calahorra, a city in Spain, embraces the martyrs Emeterius and
Chelidonius. In order to witness miracles from the power of the saints
the city often receives cures for various illnesses. These martyrs were
captured by the persecutor and bound over for punishment. After they
suffered various tortures on account of their confession of the divine
name, they welcomed the sentence of the final penalty and were led out
to be beheaded. When the executioner cut off their heads, a great
miracle appeared to the people. For the ring of one martyr and the
handkerchief of the other were taken up into a cloud and brought to
heaven. Everyone who was present saw this, and so far as the sight of
eyes could follow, the people watched the gleam of the gold [ring] and
the brightness of the linen [handkerchief] with an astonished gaze.
Aurelius Clemens [Prudentius] offers a witness for this event in these
verses from his book [entitled] "The crowns". He wrote:

"This honor is not hidden and does not grow old with time,
how the gifts that they sent up flew through the air
and demonstrate by their gleam that the road to heaven lies open.

---

[104] Felix was thought to have been martyred in the early fourth century: see
Rouche (1979) 310-11, for his cult in Gaul. Alaric II was king of the Visigoths
from 484 until his death in battle against Clovis in 507 [*HF* II.37]; although he
was an Arian, his catholic subjects in Gaul may well have supported him: see
Wood (1985) 257-8. One such catholic was Leo, a Gaul noted for his learning in
law, his eloquence, and his poetry, who had also advised Alaric's predecessor,
king Euric: see *PLRE* II:662-3, and Heinzelmann (1982) 635. Perhaps a tower
on the church at Narbonne had obstructed the king's view: see Vieillard-
Troiekouroff (1976) 189-90, and Weidemann (1982) II:136.

The ring that represented the faith of one was carried up in a cloud;
the other, as they say, gave a handkerchief as the pledge of his lips.
These gifts were seized by a celestial breeze and entered the depths
   of light.
The gleam of gold disappeared in the vault of the clear heavens;
the white fabric escaped the eyes that for long followed it.
The gifts were carried all the way to the stars and were seen no
   more."[105]

93. The martyr Cyprian of Carthage.

Cyprian, both the blessed bishop of Carthage and a martyr, often
offers assistance to ill people who request his aid. In his church is a
pulpit on which a book is placed for singing and reading. It is said to
be wonderfully built. For the whole pulpit is said to have been
sculpted from a single piece of marble. On top is a table to which one
climbs on four steps; around it are railings; below are columns. It also
has a platform beneath which eight people can take shelter. This pulpit
could never have been constructed with such craftsmanship if the power
of the martyr had not assisted.[106]

94. The Seven Sleepers at Ephesus.

Here is an account of seven brothers who are buried at Ephesus.
During the reign of the emperor Decius when there was a persecution
against the Christians, seven men were captured and brought before the
emperor. These seven men were named Maximianus, Malchus,
Martinianus, Constantinus, Dionysius, Johannes, and Serapion.
Although they were tempted by various suggestions to yield, they never
acquiesced. Because of his regard for them the emperor granted time to
think, so that they would not die immediately. But the seven men shut
themselves up in one cave, and there they lived for many days. One of
them would leave, purchase supplies, and bring back necessities. When
the emperor returned to Ephesus, the seven men requested of the Lord

[105] Few reliable details about Emeterius and Celedonius are available.
Gregory here quoted Prudentius, *Peristephanon* 1.82-90, ed. and trans.
H.J.Thomson, LCL (1949-1953) II:104-5.
[106] Bishop Cyprian of Carthage had acquired prominence as a theologian
before suffering martyrdom in 258: see Sage (1975).

that he deign to rescue them from this danger. They prayed, and while bowed to the ground they fell asleep. When the emperor learned that they were staying in this cave, by the will of God he ordered that the mouth of the cave be blocked off with huge stones. He said: "Let those who refuse to sacrifice to our gods die there." While this was being done, a Christian wrote the names of the martyrs on a lead tablet and secretly put it in the entrance to the cave before it was blocked off. After many years had gone by and peace had been granted to the churches, Theodosius, a Christian, became emperor. The impure heresy of the Sadducees, who denied that there would be a resurrection, was spreading. Then a citizen of Ephesus who decided to use this mountain as a sheepfold for his flocks overturned stones for the construction of walls for his pens. Not knowing what had happened within, he opened the entrance to the cave; but he did not find the inner chamber that was further inside. The Lord sent the breath of life to the seven men and they awoke. Thinking that they had been asleep for only one night, they sent a young man from their number to purchase food. When the young man came to the gate of the city, he was surprised upon seeing an image of the glorious cross and hearing the people take oaths in the name of Christ. As soon as he presented the coins that he had from the reign of Decius, a merchant seized him and said: "You have found a hoard that was buried years ago." The young man denied [the accusation] and was brought to the bishop and the judge of the city, who denounced him. Compelled by force the young man revealed the hidden mystery and brought them to the cave where the other men were. As the bishop entered, he found the lead tablet on which everything the men had endured was recorded in writing. The bishop spoke with the men; then the bishop and the judge quickly announced this news to the emperor Theodosius. The emperor came and honored them by kneeling on the ground. The seven men spoke to the same emperor with these words: "A heresy has spread, glorious Augustus, that attempts to mislead the Christian people from the promises of God by saying that there is no resurrection of the dead. Therefore, because, as you know, we will all be held responsible before the tribunal of Christ in accordance with what the apostle Paul wrote [cf. II Corinthians 5:10], the Lord has ordered us to be awakened and to say these things to you. Take care lest you be seduced and excluded from the kingdom of God." The emperor Theodosius listened and glorified the Lord who did not allow his people to perish. But the men again lay down on the ground and fell asleep.

When the emperor Theodosius wished to construct tombs of gold for them, he was warned in a vision not to do so. Even today the men lie asleep in that spot, covered by cloaks made of silk or linen. The record of their suffering, which with the assistance of a Syrian I translated into Latin, gives a fuller account.[107]

95. The forty-eight martyrs who suffered in Armenia.

Some say that in Armenia there were forty-eight men who suffered in the Armenian mountains where the land is gripped by hard frozen ice because of the great altitude.[108] The lawgiver [Moses] reveals the great height of these mountains when he writes that the ark that Noah built came to rest on top of them [cf. Genesis 8:4]. In these mountains a persecutor dug up the ground and constructed a huge cistern that he ordered filled with water. He then ordered that the men be stripped and their hands tied behind their backs and that they be placed on the lake

---

[107] Decius was emperor from 249 to 251, Theodosius II from 408 to 450. In New Testament times the Sadducees had been members of a priestly class in Judaism who had denied the resurrection of the body. Gregory now apparently applied the label to all who thought likewise; once he debated with a priest who had been "poisoned by the evilness of the Sadducees" [HF X.13]. For Gregory's longer account of the Seven Sleepers, see his *Passio sanctorum martyrum septem dormientium apud Ephysum*, ed. B.Krusch, *MGH*, SRM 1.2 (1885) 848-53, and again in SRM 7 (1920) 761-9; and trans. McDermott (1975) 199-206. At the end of this *Passio* Gregory named his Syrian assistant as Johannes, who may also have helped Gregory read other Greek sources: see Krusch (1885) 461. For a summary of the complexities of the archaeology of the Grotto of the Seven Sleepers, see Foss (1979) 42-3, 84-6; Honigmann (1953) speculates ingeniously on the possible historical events behind the story.

[108] Gregory was certainly referring here to the Forty Martyrs of Sebaste, thought to have been martyred in the early fourth century and much venerated in the East. It is not obvious why he claimed there had been forty-eight martyrs; perhaps he considered it appropriate to make this group of martyrs the eastern equivalents of the forty-eight martyrs of Lyon [GM 48]. Gregory probably heard this story from the "bishop from across the sea" named Simon who arrived at Tours in 591. Simon claimed to have been captured by the Persians in Armenia; he also said that the Persians had been unable to burn down the church dedicated to these Armenian martyrs [HF X.24]. Other possible sources include envoys to and from the imperial court at Constantinople or merchants: see Wood (forthcoming), who also discusses the confusion that arose over this cult in the early medieval West.

that had frozen over. A bath was kept warm opposite [the lake]. The persecutor said: "Choose one of two options. Either confess your Christ and die in this cold, or deny Christ, offer sacrifice to the gods, and run to the bath so that you can live and not miserably die for a man who was crucified." When all the men refused to sacrifice to demons, a guard saw forty-eight precious crowns falling from heaven and descending over the heads of the men. He also saw one of the crowns being recalled. For the faith of one man was weak, and as soon as guards had been left, he ran swiftly to the bath. After sacrificing victims this man was honored by the magistrate and bathed in the warm bath; but in the future he will receive the punishment of everlasting fire. One guard, as I said, saw this, and with a loud cry he announced that he was a Christian. He said: "I wish to die with these men." Immediately he was subjected to various tortures, stripped of his clothes although not of his faith, and placed on the lake. He suffered from the cold with the other men, but he will receive the crown that that wretch lost. For already the bodies of the men were dying from the cold, their teeth clattered together, and the sound of their voice was cut off. From the depths of their breast a prayer escaped to heaven only as a murmur that was heard by God alone, who knows the secrets of the heart. Their limbs trembled, wearied from fasting rather than from the frost. Their flesh had died, but their hope was directed to heaven. The unjust judge meanwhile ordered that the bath be drained and heated up seven times [hotter], so that a roaring fire might melt the men whom the cold had not weakened. Still confessing Christ the men were brought from the lake and placed among the burning vapors of the fires; but they patiently endured the tortures inflicted on them, so that they might earn a greater reward. Finally they abandoned their bodies in these [flames], transferred their souls to Christ, and consummated their martyrdom in peace. The magistrate realized that their resolve had defeated him. But since he thought that after their deaths he could overcome men whom he had not been able to overcome while they were alive, he ordered their bodies to be burned and thrown in a nearby river. When this was done, an unexpected miracle appeared to the weeping Christians. The water resisted and did not soak up the burned bodies, but instead carried them on top, as if the bodies had been favored. And so the Christians happily collected the bodies that they buried with appropriate honor.

96. The martyr Sergius.

The martyr Sergius also worked many miracles for people by healing illnesses and curing the weaknesses of those who faithfully prayed to him. As a result it happened that thereafter people either made vows or brought gifts to his large church. It is not permitted that any at all of these gifts be removed or taken away. If anyone does so, he soon pays the penalty of disgrace or of death. Because of this protection many people dedicated their possessions to the saint, so that they might be protected by his power and not be seized by evil men. Once there was an old woman who was impoverished and, I think, similar to that poor woman in the Gospel who, although she had nothing else, piously threw two mites into the offertory box [cf. Luke 21:1-2]. This woman had a few chickens among her fowl that she entrusted to the authority of the church because of a vow [she had made] to bring them to the saint's house when circumstances demanded. When many people gathered for the festival of the saint, two men who had once seen these chickens made an agreement and secretly stole one. They cut off its head, plucked its feathers, cut off its feet, and put it in a pot with water that they hung over a fire and rapidly heated. The water boiled furiously, but the stolen meat was not cooked. Even though the water boiled away, this chicken did not become tender at all. They repeatedly tested it with their hands and tried to break a claw, but they discovered that what they had put [in the water] was even tougher. Meanwhile the guests they had invited to dinner were arriving. These guests were about to receive nothing from the preparations. The table was ready, covered with white napkins and decorated with an embroidered cloth. But the food had been transformed into an unexpected toughness. Although the pot was often filled with water, nothing they put in it was found to be cooked. So, because of this unexpected miracle, the dinner was turned into stone, the hosts were dismayed, the guests were embarrassed, and everyone left the meal in shame.[109]

---

[109] Sergius was thought to have been martyred at the beginning of the fourth century. This church was presumably the one in honor of St Sergius at Sergiopolis (R'safah) in Syria: see Krautheimer (1965) 113-5, and Vieillard-Troiekouroff (1976) 431. Bishop Bertramn of Bordeaux [cf. *GM* 33] was once so impressed upon hearing about the power of the thumb of St Sergius that he tried to acquire relics of the saint [*HF* VII.31]; Gregory himself dedicated a new

97. The martyrs Cosmas and Damianus.

Cosmas and Damianus, the two twins, were skilled doctors. After they became Christians, they cured the illnesses of sick people solely by the merit of their powers and by the intervention of prayers. They were perfected by various tortures and reunited in heaven, and they now display many miracles to the local inhabitants. For whenever an ill person who is filled with faith prays at their tomb, immediately he receives medicine. Many say that the saints appear to ill people in visions and tell them what to do; once people follow these instructions, they leave with their health. I have heard from these people [who were cured] many stories that I decided would take too much time to follow up. I think that what I have said can suffice. All who pray faithfully have left with their health.[110]

98. The martyr St Phocas.

The martyr Phocas came from the same region as these martyrs [Cosmas and Damianus]. Phocas is buried in Syria. Still today it is made apparent to the people how, after he suffered many insults on behalf of the name of the Redeemer, he triumphed over that ancient serpent. For if in those regions a snake has bitten someone and injected poisons, as soon as the person who has been bitten touches the entrance to the courtyard where the martyr is buried, the tumor goes down, the infection of the poison vanishes, and the person is healed. According to a widespread report, some of these people are already distended from the bite of the evil beast and their entire bodies are already swollen from the poison that is growing in them, so that they might breathe out their lives. But when they are carried by [others'] hands and placed in the courtyard, they are cured. It is not possible for a man to die from this venom if he is filled with faith and touches the holy threshold.[111]

------

baptistry near the church of St Martin at Tours with relics of St Sergius [*HF* X.31].

[110] Cosmas and Damianus were thought to have been martyred in the early fourth century; as physicians they were honored for having collected no fees. Gregory placed relics of St Cosmas and St Damianus in the room off the cathedral of Tours that Martin had once used [*HF* X.31]

[111] Phocas was thought to have been martyred at Antioch in the early fourth century.

99. The martyr Domitius.

Domitius is another martyr from this region who, although he offers many blessings to the local inhabitants, with his quick power heals those suffering from hip pains. For the saint is said to have been hampered by this hip pain when he was alive in the flesh. Since, as I said, he heals many who ache from this affliction, a Jew who suffered from this infirmity piously went to the saint's church, even though he did not believe in Christ. He asked to be brought to the entrance of the courtyard and cried that he was unworthy to cross the holy threshold. He said: "I know, glorious martyr, that I with whom you refuse to share your compassion am blinded by the veil of the law. But now I take refuge with you and as a suppliant beg for your compassion, so that after first removing the illness of my body you might remove the illness of my unbelief." After he said this in front of the gate of the courtyard, night came and he fell asleep. But the blessed martyr did not postpone his compassion for long. During that night he approached the ill man in a dream and ordered him to depart with his health. The Jew awoke and realized that he had been restored to health. He confessed that Christ, the Son of God, was the Saviour of the world and he left with his health. When the Christians who suffered from the same infirmity saw this, they complained to the saint and said: "Behold, we who faithfully believe in God do not deserve to be freed [from our infirmities], but this man who does not believe in Christ the king and who is circumcised in the flesh but not in his heart departs with his health!" And as they said this, they began angrily to smash the lights of the church that were hanging from the rafters. But the compassion they demanded was not lacking for these people; for on that very day they were cured and returned to their own homes.[112]

100. The martyr Georgius.

I know many miracle stores about the martyr Georgius, of which I will narrate a few. Some people were carrying his relics along with the relics of other saints. When these couriers came to a place in the territory of Limoges where a few clerics had already constructed an oratory

---

[112] Domitius was thought to have been martyred in the mid-fourth century.

from wood planks and were constantly praying to the Lord, they requested lodging. They were received with kindness and they spent the night chanting psalms with the other brothers. At daybreak they took the reliquary but could not lift it at all. Since they completely refused to travel without the holy relics, a great grief came into their hearts. They understood, by the inspiration of God, that they ought to leave some of their relics in this place. They searched in the fastenings [around the relics] and cut off some pieces; they presented them to the elder [cleric] who presided at the oratory. By leaving a part of their protection they received the opportunity of departing to where they wished to go.

There are relics of Georgius in the village [of Saint-Martin-des-Bois in the territory] of Le Mans, where often many miracles are revealed. For the blind, the lame, those with chills, and other ill people are often there rewarded with the favor of health.[113]

101. The martyr Isiodorus.

The martyr Isiodorus is buried on the island of Chios—such is the name of the island. In the saint's church there is a well into which he is said to have been thrown. After drinking from the water of this well possessed people, people with fevers, and other ill people are often cured. It is said that believers often see there a light similar to a burning candle. I myself met a priest who insisted that he had often seen this light [shining] from the mouth of the well. On this island a seed is picked from the mastic trees that, so they widely say, are not found in other regions.[114]

102. The martyr Polyeuctus.

The martyr Polyeuctus, although he is noted for great miracles, is venerated with a great cult at Constantinople for this reason especially,

---

[113] Georgius was thought to have been martyred in the early fourth century in Palestine; he was eventually transformed into the St George noted for having killed a dragon. The precise location of the oratory near Limoges is unknown, and the shrine near Le Mans is conjectured to be at Saint-Martin-des-Bois: see Vieillard-Troiekouroff (1976) 265, 353.

[114] Isiodorus (or Isidorus) was thought to have been martyred in the mid-third century.

that he takes immediate vengeance against perjurers. For whoever commits, as often happens, a secret crime and, after being put under suspicion, is brought to this church, either he is frightened by the power of the martyr and immediately confesses what he did, or, if he commits perjury, he is immediately struck down by divine vengeance. Juliana, a woman from Constantinople, covered the ceiling of this church with pure gold, in this fashion. When a report of her wealth was recounted by many people and reached the emperor Justinian, he did not hesitate to hurry swiftly to meet her. He said: "O venerable mother, I think that you are not unaware how the public treasuries are empty of gold coins at a time when we wish you to be at peace, when we intend to defend the country, when we reconcile the barbarians to ourselves, and when we seek to compensate various people with gifts. Therefore, because the power of the divine majesty has given you much gold, I ask that you extend your hand to us and donate some money. Then, when the total of the public taxes is announced, what you have lent will be instantly returned to you. In the future, when the fame of your renown spreads, people will chant that the matron Juliana has supported Constantinople with her wealth." But she saw through the deception of the emperor and wisely concealed what she had dedicated to God. She said: "My small income, both what is expected from rents as well as what is expected from harvests, remains still at my homes. If therefore you in your glory will permit a delay in receiving it, it will be presented for your inspection once it has been collected. And when you have seen everything with your own eyes, you may discard or take whatever is pleasing. I will do whatever the desire of your heart decides." The emperor was tricked by these words. He happily returned to his palace and thought that he already had this money in the public treasuries. But Juliana gathered some craftsmen and secretly gave them whatever gold she could find in her storerooms. She said: "Go, construct plates to fit the measure of the beams, and decorate the ceiling [of the church] of the blessed martyr Polyeuctus with this gold, so that the hand of this greedy emperor cannot touch these things." The craftsmen completed everything that the woman ordered by attaching [the plates] to the ceiling and covering it with pure gold. Once the task was finished, the woman summoned the emperor and said: "The little bit of my money that I could collect is here. Come to see it, and do what you wish." The emperor happily rose from his throne; but he was to receive none of the gold. He came to the woman's house intending to transport great treasures back to his palace. When the woman humbly met him, she invited him to pray in the church of the martyr that was next to her house. For she had dedicated whatever she could possess to that holy place. The emperor took Juliana's hand because she was an old woman, entered the church, and knelt for prayer. When his prayer was over, the woman said: "Most glorious Augustus, I ask that you look at the ceiling of this church and realize that my poorness is kept there in this craftsmanship. But you now do what you wish. I will not oppose you." The emperor looked up, was surprised, and then was embarrassed. In order to conceal his shame he praised the craftsmanship, gave thanks, and prepared to leave. But so that the emperor not return empty-handed, the woman removed a ring from her finger but concealed the jewel in her palm. The ring contained no more than half an ounce of gold. Juliana offered the ring to the emperor and said: "Most hallowed emperor, receive from my hand this small gift that is assessed at more than the value of this gold." For in the ring was a Neronian emerald, very green and shiny. When the emerald was exposed, it seemed that the beauty of the jewel had somehow transformed all the gold [on the ceiling] into greenness. The emperor received the ring, repeatedly gave thanks and praised the woman, and then returned to his palace. As a result there is no doubt that the power of the martyr had intervened in this affair to prevent the wealth that had been given to this holy place and to the poor from being transferred to the control of this emperor who had not exerted himself in collecting it.[115]

[115] Polyeuctus was thought to have been martyred in the mid-third century. Anicia Juliana was a member of a most distinguished family; from the late fourth to the mid-fifth century several of her ancestors had been emperors in the West: see *PLRE* II:635-6. Much of this church dedicated to St Polyeuctus was constructed during the period from 524 to 527, that is, before Justinian became emperor in 527 and during the reign of his uncle, Justin I: see Harrison (1986). At the time patronage for this church may have been intended as a reaffirmation of the importance of Juliana's family in the face of these upstart emperors. But by passing on this ring to Justinian Juliana may also have been tacitly conceding the transfer of imperial power to another dynasty: see Harrison (1983). King Childebert and king Guntramn once guaranteed a treaty by invoking the names of St Hilary and St Martin, two great Gallic saints, and of St Polyeuctus, who was noted for his vengeance on perjurers [*HF* VII.6].

103. The martyr Felix of Nola.

Because no account of the suffering of Felix, a martyr at Nola, is available, it is a pleasure to include in this chapter a few stories corresponding to that which the blessed Paulinus [of Nola] recorded in verse.[116] Felix was rewarded with the honor of a priesthood by Maximus, bishop of the aforementioned city [of Nola]. The excellence of his wisdom and his erudition could not be concealed either from Christians or from pagans. But when decrees of emperors ordered a persecution of Christians, bishop Maximus, who was already weighed down by old age and thought he could not endure tortures, hid in the ravines of the forests. Upset by the persecution he wandered through the ravines; weakened by hunger, worn down by the cold, he fell to the ground half dead. But the priest Felix was captured. Because he had argued that many omens of the gods were of no value, he endured various types of tortures and was condemned to prison. Although confined [in prison], he was not bound by these flimsy chains. For in the middle of the night an angel of the Lord came to him, broke the chains, and cut the stocks that confined his feet. The angel said: "Rise and follow me." Felix rose and with the angel passed through the door of the prison. The angel of the Lord said to him: "Climb into the mountains and find your bishop. After you find and revive him, bring him to the city and hide him in a secret place, so that he does not die from starvation and hardship until the persecution of Christians is over." Felix accepted this mandate and set out to a place he did not know. But due to the providence of God he found the bishop lying on the ground, his eyes closed and his teeth clenched. No more than faint breathing kept him alive. When Felix addressed him, he could elicit no response; when Felix touched him, he felt that the bishop's limbs were

---

[116] Felix was thought to have suffered probably during one of the persecutions of the third century. In the later fourth century Paulinus, a Gallic aristocrat from Aquitaine who had already served in the imperial administration, moved to Nola, where he eventually served as bishop until his death in 431: see Frend (1969), Brown (1981) 53-68, and Van Dam (1985) 303-11. Paulinus wrote a series of poems in honor of St Felix whom he adopted as one of his patron saints: ed. G.de Hartel, *CSEL* 30 (1894), and trans. P.G.Walsh, ACW 40 (1975). Gregory much admired Paulinus [*GC* 108], and in this chapter he used excerpts from four of his poems about St Felix.

frozen by the winter and almost dead, without the warmth of life. Felix worried because there was no food that he might give to the bishop who was in danger; nor did he have the means to kindle a fire. While Felix stood there confounded, he saw the gift of an angel that had fallen, as it were, from the heavenly abode in this manner. For behold, he noted that hanging from a nearby thicket was a cluster whose grapes he squeezed into the mouth of the confessor Maximus. In a bit the old man revived and stood up. After lifting Maximus on his shoulders Felix returned with such speed that he was thought to be carried rather than to be carrying. He entrusted the bishop to the cottage of a widow and brought food until the persecution of the Christians was over. After the bishop died, Felix was elected by the people to preside over the throne of the church, but he was unwilling to agree; so a priest named Quintus was consecrated bishop. A persecution of catholics arose. When the priest Felix warned the people in the street not to deviate from the correct path, a persecutor unfamiliar with the priest Felix was sent. The persecutor began to ask who Felix was. Pointing with his right hand Felix said: "He lives over there." When the persecutor left, Felix looked for a hiding place. After entering through a small door he wished to hide himself among the ruined walls. Immediately the persecutor followed; but God tricked the zeal of the pursuer. For at the command of the Divinity spiders wove strands of webs over the door by which the martyr had entered. When those who followed his footprints attempted to investigate the place, they noted the beginnings of a web and said to each other: "Do you think that a man crossed through these threads that often the light weight of flies breaks?" They left after being tricked by the providence of God. When night came the blessed Felix went to another place where for three months he received the sustenance of food from a woman. When peace came, he was restored to his church and the people. But while he waited in his hiding place he never saw the face of the woman who cared for him, and she never saw his. After he died in peace, he was buried next to the city. He reveals himself among the people through many miracles, of which I will mention a few.

A poor man had two oxen for working in his field. He owned nothing else, except what he was able to work at with these oxen by cutting the ground with a plow. It happened that one day he was wearily returning from his work; he unhitched his oxen and disappeared into his little cottage. Immediately a greedy thief arrived who secretly took the oxen and led them away with him. The next day the poor man came out and found nothing. He looked on the back roads, circled the forests, and climbed mountain peaks; but he found not even a trace. He returned to his own home crying and weeping, and with his wife and children he mourned. He said: "Woe to me, because after the disappearance of our oxen you will die this year from starvation!" Why say more? Still grieving he went to the tomb of the blessed martyr Felix, he groaned and wept, and he prayed that the power of Felix might obtain from the Lord that what he had lost would be returned to him. As he left the church he saw his own oxen in front of the entrance to the courtyard. He said: "Great is the power of the martyr which caused what I had lost to be restored so quickly to me." He entered the church again, knelt on the pavement, and gave thanks; then he went home with his oxen. For the power of the martyr had also given sight to the eye of this man that had been blind.

Connected to the wall of this church where the blessed body lies buried in a tomb is an attached walkway, in which a lamp hanging on a rope usually offered light to the area. The man whose duty was to look after the maintenance of this lamp entered. After untying the rope he left to find some oil. Everything was covered and gripped by the darkness of night, and the rope with its small hooks was hanging slack in the middle of the walkway. One of those attending the vigil of the saint was wearied by the smoke in the church that arose from the burning of papyri, and he went outside. As he was passing through this walkway, one of the hooks on the rope caught at the face of the man as he passed by and with its exposed point pierced his eye. The man was in pain, and with his outstretched hands he covered his face and eyes that were in danger. He cried out in a loud voice and said: "Holy priest [Felix], I beg you to help. You who are near this place, be near to one who is dying. Extend your holy hands with a secret medicine and eliminate the misfortune that threatens my sight, lest I who came to see the light of your miracles leave without my sight." When those who were present brought a light to the tearful cries of this man, they saw the man hanging from the rope with his eye pierced. Although the blood was flowing [down his face], no one dared to raise a hand to rescue him. The overwhelming power of the blessed martyr was present, and he extracted the hook in such a way that he did not tear the eye, he did not penetrate the man's vision, but he did stop the flow of dripping blood. Once the iron [hook] was extracted from the man's eye and the pain in his eyes lessened, the people witnessed the power of the holy martyr. This author [Paulinus of Nola] has written that often possessed people are tested and cleansed at the sacred church of this athlete of Christ. But let us return to the martyrs of Gaul.

104. Vincentius of Agen.

Vincentius was a martyr at Agen, and the local inhabitants have an account of his suffering. In the church of Christ Vincentius sparkles with the brightness of his deacon's robe, and very often he shines out with great miracles. He is a harsh avenger against those who invade his possessions. Once when an army was raised against Gundovald and sent to Comminges, these many enemies besieged the saint's church. The people were safe inside the church and entrusted the protection of all their possessions to respect for the martyr, because no one was presumptuous and rash enough to dare to touch them. After locking the doors they barricaded themselves inside with their possessions. The enemy surrounded the doors but could not find an opening through which they might enter; so they set fire to the doors of the church. Even after burning fiercely for a long time the doors were not taken until smashed by the blows of axes. The enemy entered, seized the possessions, and slaughtered the people inside with the edge of their swords. But not for long did this deed remain unavenged. Some of these men were possessed by a demon, some drowned in the Garonne river, many were stricken by a chill; in different ways they were afflicted by different types of diseases. For I saw in the territory of Tours many of those who had been involved in this crime. They were painfully destroyed and suffered to the end of their present lives from the torture of excruciating pains. Many of them confessed that because of the insult to the martyr they had been destined by the judgement of God for a horrible death. Behold how God provides for his martyrs! Behold with what praises Christ, the Lord and overseer of pious wars, honors them! Behold how distinguished is the dignity of that Christian name, so long as we do not imitate unbelievers in giving in to greed and serving luxury![117]

[117] This Vincentius of Agen was probably an apocryphal martyr and may well have been invented as a local double of the better known Vincentius of Saragossa [*GM* 89]: see Griffe (1964-1966) I:141. The *Passio* that Gregory

105. The woman who hoarded money.

I have heard about something that happened years ago in Gaul. Under the guise of religious sincerity a woman devoted herself to fasting, applied herself to praying, kept vigils without fail, and, pretending to be pious, often visited the holy shrines. Because she persisted in the appearance of a just life, she acquired much wealth from many people. Everyday she collected gold, and what Christians in their piety offered for ransoming prisoners she hid in secret places. Whatever was given as a benefit for the dire straits of the poor she concealed in her wicked moneybags. The woman dug out the earth and put an enormous jar in the middle of her cell, and whenever something was given her she carefully put it there [in the jar]. To prevent anyone from finding her secret [cache] she covered it with a stone on top. O greediness, three and four times to be cursed, you who cheat men of the light and plunge them into darkness! Why say more? When the jar was filled with coins, the moment of revelation came for this woman. She died [before] God, migrated to the underworld, and was buried. After her funeral the clerics who were present asked her servant girl what the woman had done with so much money and whether there had been sufficient time for her to spend it. The servant girl replied that she had never seen the woman extend a hand of compassion to any poor person. She admitted that she did not know what had happened to the money that had been given to the woman. She said: "I know only this one fact, that I never saw anything that was taken into the cell brought outside again." As the clerics listened they were surprised at what they heard, and they carefully inquired about what had become of the money. They repeatedly tapped on the floor. The spot where the money lay hidden returned an echo of the blow and with a hollow sound it revealed what was hidden. Immediately they removed the stone and found the

---

mentioned may still be extant: see de Gaiffier (1952), and Griffe (1956). Gundovald was a Gallic painter [*HF* VII.36] who pretended to be a son of king Chlothar and eventually acquired support from both bishops and Frankish magistrates. In 585 king Guntramn initiated a campaign against Gundovald, who was finally betrayed and murdered. As part of his account of this expedition Gregory essentially repeated this story about the desecration of the church of St Vincentius [*HF* VII.35]. This church was located at Le Mas d'Agenais: see Vieillard-Troiekouroff (1976) 166-7.

pile of gold. The clerics were stunned at the perversity of such ingenuity and asked the bishop what had been done. The bishop was upset
and ordered the woman's tomb to be opened and the money thrown on
top of her lifeless body. He said: "What you have collected for yourself is to be yours; the poor of Christ will not lack sustenance."
Shortly afterwards when people first fell asleep during the night shouts
were heard from the tomb along with crying and loud screams. In the
midst of this shouting this [cry] especially echoed out, that she who
was being consumed by molten gold was a miserable wretch. After
these shouts had gone on for three days at nightfall, the people could
not tolerate them and went to the bishop. The bishop came and ordered
the lid of the tomb to be removed. When the lid was removed, he saw
that the gold, as if it had been melted in a furnace, had trickled into the
woman's mouth along with its sulphurous flame. Then the bishop
prayed to the Lord that, since the woman's evilness had been exposed to
the people, the Lord should order the punishment of her body to stop.
After the tomb was covered, he left. The woman's shouts were no
longer heard.

You see, therefore, what a distinction there is between life in
heaven and the wealth of this world, and between the riches of the
martyrs and the trappings of this world. You see what rewards are
conferred upon the martyrs as compensation for a devout life. O mortal
man, you do not shrink from crimes, you do not desist from vices, you
do not struggle against fierce desires! Your eye seduces you when you
look at others' possessions, although a generous donation of riches did
not corrupt the holy martyr. You are tossed about by wicked thoughts
and you yield to them, although the martyr did not yield to fires and
instruments of torture. One prick from an evil desire wounds you,
although neither a whirlwind of words nor the gallows could deflect a
martyr of Christ from the path of righteousness. The martyr endured
these torments in a visible body like yours, and you do not restrain the
invisible agitations of the body. As the apostle wrote, the flesh lusts
against the spirit and the spirit against the flesh, and both in turn are
opposed to each other [cf. Galatians 5:17], so that we do that which we
do not wish. Consider nevertheless what the same teacher writes: "I
see in my limbs a law at war with the law of my mind and making me
captive to the law of sin" [Romans 7:23]. Therefore, if you feel that
you are being led captive to the law of sin, protect your forehead with

the illustrious sign of the cross. With it you can deflect the prick of this treachery, as Prudentius writes:
"The cross repels every crime,
and darkness flees from the cross.
Consecrated with such a sign
the mind does not know how to bend."[118]
I will narrate something that happened recently [to demonstrate] how much strength there is in this most holy standard [of the cross].

106. The insolence of a fly that was turned aside by the sign of a bishop.

In the territory of Poitiers a priest named Pannichius asked for a cup when he sat down at a banquet with the friends whom he had invited. After he received it, an annoying fly buzzed around and tried to contaminate the cup. The priest often shooed the fly away with his hand. When the fly again flew up and tried to return, the priest knew that it was a trick of the enemy. He took the cup in his left hand and made the sign of the cross with his right hand. The cup shattered into four pieces, and the liquid in it, after a wave had been tossed in the air, was spilled on the ground. For it was very obvious that this was a trick of the enemy.

So also you, if you manfully and firmly place the sign of salvation on your forehead or your chest, then by resisting vices you will be considered a martyr. For the martyrs themselves achieved their victories not by their own strength but with the assistance of God through the most glorious sign of the cross. As I have often said, the Lord himself struggles and triumphs in the martyrs. Therefore it is necessary for us to seek the patronage of the martyrs, so that we might be worthy to be helped by their assistance. What we are not worthy to obtain by our own merits, we can receive by their intercessions. Hence, by using the aid of the sacred Trinity and by rejecting the desires of the flesh we are worthy to become martyrs, as was said by him who crowns with precious jewels in heaven those who faithfully struggle for him [cf. I Peter 2:11]. He deigns to protect in this world the foster children who respect his friends. He ensures that the martyrs whom he receives after

---

[118] Quoted from Prudentius, *Cathemerinon* 6.133-6, ed. and trans. H.J.Thomson, LCL (1949-1953) I:56-7.

their victory as immortals in the beauty of Paradise will be of assistance when invoked by his people. At the moment of judgement when
eternal glory surrounds the martyrs, either the mercy of their mediation
will excuse us or a lenient penalty will pass over us. In a trial for a
crime the Lord will not condemn to eternity defendants whom he has
redeemed with the price of [the martyrs'] precious blood.

BIBLIOGRAPHY

Antin, P. (1963). "Autour du songe de S. Jérôme," *Revue des études latines* 41, pp.350-77. Reprinted in his *Recueil sur saint Jérôme*. Collection Latomus 95 (Brussels, 1968) 71-100.

Auerbach, E. (1953). *Mimesis. The representation of reality in western literature*, trans. W.R.Trask (Princeton).

Bachrach, B.S. (1977). *Early medieval Jewish policy in western Europe* (Minneapolis).

Baus, K., H.-G.Beck, E.Ewig, and H.J.Vogt (1980). *The imperial Church from Constantine to the early Middle Ages. = History of the Church*, ed. H.Jedin and J.Dolan, vol.2, trans. A.Biggs (New York).

Baynes, N.H. (1929). [review of books by Lot, Pirenne, and Rostovtzeff], *Journal of Roman Studies* 19, pp.224-35. Partially reprinted in his *Byzantine studies and other essays* (London, 1955) 307-16.

van Berchem, D. (1956). *Le martyre de la Legion Thébaine. Essai sur la formation d'une légende* (Basel).

Biraben, J.-N. and J.Le Goff (1975). "The plague in the early Middle Ages," in *Biology of man in history*, ed. R.Forster and O.Ranum, trans. E.Forster and P.M.Ranum (Baltimore) 48-80.

Blumenkranz, B. (1960). *Juifs et Chrétiens dans le monde occidental 430-1096* (Paris).

Bonnet, M. (1890). *Le Latin de Grégoire de Tours* (Paris).

Bornkamm, G. (1965). "The Acts of Thomas," in E.Hennecke, *New Testament Apocrypha*, ed. W.Schneemelcher, vol.2. English translation ed. R.McL.Wilson (Philadelphia) 425-41.

Brennan, B. (1985). "The career of Venantius Fortunatus," *Traditio* 41, pp.49-78.

———. (1985a). "The conversion of the Jews of Clermont in AD 576," *Journal of Theological Studies* n.s.36, pp.321-37.

———. (1985b). "Senators and social mobility in sixth-century Gaul," *Journal of Medieval History* 11, pp.145-61.

Brown, P. (1981). *The cult of the saints. Its rise and function in Latin Christianity* (Chicago).

Buchner, R. (1955). "Einleitung," in *Gregor von Tours, Zehn Bücher Geschichten*, ed. and trans. R.Buchner (Darmstadt, 4th ed.) I: VII-LI.

Cameron, Av. (1975). "The Byzantine sources of Gregory of Tours," *Journal of Theological Studies* n.s.26, pp.421-6. Reprinted in her *Continuity and change in sixth-century Byzantium* (London, 1981), Chap.XV.

_____. (1976). "The early religious policies of Justin II," in *The orthodox churches and the West*, ed. D.Baker. *Studies in Church History* 13 (Oxford) 51-67. Reprinted in her *Continuity and change in sixth-century Byzantium* (London, 1981), Chap.X.

_____. (1978). "The Theotokos in sixth-century Constantinople. A city finds its symbol," *Journal of Theological Studies* n.s.29, pp.79-108. Reprinted in her *Continuity and change in sixth-century Byzantium* (London, 1981), Chap.XVI.

Cavallin, S. (1945). "Saint Genès le notaire," *Eranos* 43, pp.150-75.

Chadwick, H. (1981). *Boethius. The consolations of music, logic, theology, and philosophy* (Oxford).

Chadwick, O. (1948). "Gregory of Tours and Gregory the Great," *Journal of Theological Studies* 49, pp.38-49.

Clark, E.A. (1982). "Claims on the bones of Saint Stephen: the partisans of Melania and Eudocia," *Church History* 51, pp.141-56. Reprinted in her *Ascetic piety and women's faith. Essays on late ancient Christianity*. Studies in Women and Religion 20 (Lewiston, 1986) 95-123.

Collins, R. (1980). "Mérida and Toledo: 550-585," in *Visigothic Spain: new approaches*, ed. E.James (Oxford) 189-219.

_____. (1983). *Early medieval Spain: unity in diversity, 400-1000* (London).

Courcelle, P. (1964). *Histoire littéraire des grandes invasions germaniques* (Paris, 3rd ed.).

Courtois, C. (1955). *Les Vandales et l'Afrique* (Paris).

Dagron, G. (1974). *Naissance d'une capitale. Constantinople et ses institutions de 330 à 451* (Paris).

Dalton, O.M. (1927). *The history of the Franks by Gregory of Tours* (Oxford), 2 vols. [I: Introduction; II: Translation and notes].

Dassmann, E. (1975). "Ambrosius und die Märtyrer," *Jahrbuch für Antike und Christentum* 18, pp.49-68.

Delehaye, H. (1927). *Sanctus. Essai sur le culte des saints dans l'antiquité.* Subsidia hagiographica 17 (Brussels).

_____. (1933). *Les origines du culte des martyrs.* Subsidia hagiographica 20 (Brussels, 2nd ed.).

Drake, H.A. (1985). "Eusebius on the True Cross," *Journal of Ecclesiastical History* 36, pp.1-22.

Duchesne, L. (1894-1915). *Fastes épiscopaux de l'ancienne Gaule* (Paris), 3 vols.

Dupraz, L. (1961). *Les Passions de S. Maurice d'Agaune. Essai sur l'historicité de la tradition et contribution à l'étude de l'armée pré-Dioclétienne (260-286) et des canonisations tardives de la fin du IVᵉ siècle* (Fribourg).

Dvornik, F. (1958). *The idea of apostolicity in Byzantium and the legend of the Apostle Andrew* (Cambridge, Massachusetts).

van Esbroeck, M. (1981). "Les textes littéraires sur l'Assomption avant le Xᵉ siècle," in *Les Actes apocryphes des apôtres. Christianisme et monde païen,* ed. F.Bovon et al. (Geneva) 265-85.

Ewig, E. (1960). "Die Kathedralpatrozinien im römischen und im fränkischen Gallien," *Historisches Jahrbuch* 79, pp.1-61. Reprinted in his *Spätantikes und fränkisches Gallien. Gesammelte Schriften (1952-1973),* ed. H.Atsma, vol.2 (Munich, 1979) 260-317.

_____. (1960a). "Der Petrus- und Apostelkult im spätrömischen und fränkischen Gallien," *Zeitschrift für Kirchengeschichte* 71, pp.215-51. Reprinted in his *Spätantikes und fränkisches Gallien. Gesammelte Schriften (1952-1973),* ed. H.Atsma, vol.2 (Munich, 1979) 318-54.

_____. (1964). "Die Verehrung orientalischer Heiliger im spätrömischen Gallien und im Merowingerreich," in *Festschrift Percy Ernst Schramm,* vol.1 (Wiesbaden) 385-400. Reprinted in his *Spätantikes und fränkisches Gallien. Gesammelte Schriften (1952-1973),* ed. H.Atsma, vol.2 (Munich, 1979) 393-410.

Foss, C. (1979). *Ephesus after antiquity: a late antique Byzantine and Turkish city* (Cambridge).

Frend, W.H.C. (1965). *Martyrdom and persecution in the early Church* (Oxford).

_____. (1969). "Paulinus of Nola and the last century of the western empire," *Journal of Roman Studies* 59, pp.1-11. Reprinted in his *Town and country in the early Christian centuries* (London, 1980), Chap.XIV.

Frolow, A. (1961). *La relique de la Vraie Croix. Recherches sur le développement d'un culte.* Archives de l'Orient chrétien 7 (Paris).

de Gaiffier, B. (1952). "La Passion de S. Vincent d'Agen," *Analecta Bollandiana* 70, pp.160-81.

Garrod, H.W. (1919). "Virgil and Gregory of Tours," *Classical Review* 33, p.28.

Geary, P.J. (1988). *Before France and Germany. The creation and transformation of the Merovingian world* (Oxford).

Gilliard, F.D. (1975). "The apostolicity of Gallic churches," *Harvard Theological Review* 68, pp.17-33.

_____. (1979). "The senators of sixth-century Gaul," *Speculum* 54, pp.685-97.

Goffart, W. (1985). "The conversions of Avitus of Clermont, and similar passages in Gregory of Tours," in *"To see ourselves as others see us." Christians, Jews, "others" in late antiquity*, ed. J.Neusner and E.S.Frerichs (Chico) 473-97.

_____. (1987). "From *Historiae* to *Historia Francorum* and back again: aspects of the textual history of Gregory of Tours," in *Religion, culture, and society in the early Middle Ages. Studies in honor of Richard E. Sullivan*, ed. T.F.X.Noble and J.J.Contreni (Kalamazoo) 55-76.

des Graviers, J. (1946). "La date du commencement de l'année chez Grégoire de Tours," *Revue d'histoire de l'église de France* 32, pp.103-6.

Griffe, E. (1948). "Le véritable emplacement du Capitole romain de Toulouse," *Bulletin de littérature ecclésiastique* 49, pp.32-41.

_____. (1955). "Les origines chrétiennes de la Gaule et les légendes clémentines," *Bulletin de littérature ecclésiastique* 56, pp.3-22.

_____. (1956). "La Passion de saint Vincent d'Agen," *Bulletin de littérature ecclésiastique* 57, pp.98-103.

_____. (1959). "Toulouse romaine et chrétienne. Controverses et incertitudes," *Bulletin de littérature ecclésiastique* 60, pp.117-34.

_____. (1964-1966). *La Gaule chrétienne à l'époque romaine* (Paris, rev.ed.), 3 vols.

Harrison, R.M. (1983). "The Church of St. Polyeuktos in Istanbul and the temple of Solomon," in *Okeanos. Essays presented to Ihor Sevcenko on his sixtieth birthday by his colleagues and students*, ed. C.Mango and O.Pritsak, with U.M.Pasicznyk. *Harvard Ukrainian Studies* 7, pp.276-9.

_____. (1986). *Excavations at Saraçhane in Istanbul*, vol.1 (Princeton).

Heinzelmann, M. (1982). "Gallische Prosopographie 260-527," *Francia* 10, pp.531-718.

Hochstetler, D. (1987). "The meaning of monastic cloister for women according to Caesarius of Arles," in *Religion, culture, and society in the early Middle Ages. Studies in honor of Richard E. Sullivan*, ed. T.F.X.Noble and J.J.Contreni (Kalamazoo) 27-40.

Homes Dudden, F. (1935). *The life and times of St. Ambrose* (Oxford).

Honigmann, E. (1953). "Stephen of Ephesus (April 15, 448—Oct.29, 451) and the legend of the Seven Sleepers," in his *Patristic studies. Studi e testi* 173 (Vatican City) 125-68.

Hornschuh, M. (1965). "Acts of Andrew," in E.Hennecke, *New Testament Apocrypha*, ed. W.Schneemelcher, vol.2. English translation ed. R.McL.Wilson (Philadelphia) 390-403.

Hunt, E.D. (1982). *Holy Land pilgrimage in the later Roman empire AD 312-460* (Oxford).

James, E. (1982). *The origins of France. From Clovis to the Capetians, 500-1000* (New York).

_____. (1983). "'Beati pacifici': bishops and the law in sixth-century Gaul," in *Disputes and settlements. Law and human relations in the West*, ed. J.Bossy (Cambridge) 25-46.

_____. (1985), trans. *Gregory of Tours, Life of the Fathers* (Liverpool).

Kartsonis, A.D. (1986). *Anastasis. The making of an image* (Princeton).

Kelly, J.N.D. (1975). *Jerome. His life, writings, and controversies* (London).

Krautheimer, R. (1965). *Early Christian and Byzantine architecture* (Baltimore).

Krusch, B. (1885). "Georgii Florentii Gregorii episcopi Turonensis libri octo miraculorum," in *MGH*, SRM 1 (Hannover) 451-820 [Introduction, edition of text, and notes].

_____. (1920). "Appendix. Tomus I. Georgii Florentii Gregorii episcopi Turonensis libri VIII miraculorum," in *MGH*, SRM 7 (Hannover and Leipzig) 707-72

_____. (1951). "Gregorii episcopi Turonensis decem libri historiarum. Praefatio," in *MGH*, SRM 1.1, editio altera, fasc.3 (Hannover) IX-XXII.

Kurth, G. (1919). *Etudes franques* (Paris and Brussels), 2 vols.

de Lacger, L. (1927). "Saint Vincent de Saragosse," *Revue d'histoire de l'église de France* 13, pp.307-58.

Markus, R.A. (1978). "The cult of icons in sixth-century Gaul," *Journal of Theological Studies* n.s.29, pp.151-7. Reprinted in his *From Augustine to Gregory the Great. History and Christianity in late antiquity* (London, 1983), Chap.XII.

Marrou, H.I. (1970). "Le dossier épigraphique de l'évêque Rusticus de Narbonne," *Rivista di archeologia cristiana* 46, pp.331-49.

Masai, F. (1971). "La 'Vita patrum Iurensium' et les débuts du monachisme à Saint-Maurice d'Agaune," in *Festschrift Bernhard Bischoff zu seinem 65. Geburtstag dargebracht von Freunden, Kollegen und Schülern*, ed. J.Autenrieth and F.Brunhölzl (Stuttgart) 43-69.

Mathisen, R.W. (1982). "PLRE II: suggested *addenda* and *corrigenda*," *Historia* 31, pp.364-86.

McCarthy, M.C. (1960). *The Rule for nuns of St. Caesarius of Arles. A translation with a critical introduction* (Washington, D.C.).

McCulloh, J.M. (1976). "The cult of relics in the letters and 'Dialogues' of pope Gregory the Great: a lexicographical study," *Traditio* 32, pp.145-84.

McDermott, W.C. (1975). "Bishops: the world of Gregory of Tours," in *Monks, bishops and pagans. Christian culture in Gaul and Italy, 500-700*, ed. E.Peters (Philadelphia) 117-218.

Monod, G. (1872). *Etudes critiques sur les sources de l'histoire mérovingienne*, vol.1 (Paris).

de Nie, G. (1985). "The spring, the seed and the tree: Gregory of Tours on the wonders of nature," *Journal of Medieval History* 11, pp.89-135. Reprinted in her *Views from a many-windowed tower. Studies of imagination in the works of Gregory of Tours* (Amsterdam, 1987) 71-132.

Pelikan, J. (1971). *The emergence of the catholic tradition (100-600)*. = *The Christian tradition. A history of the development of doctrine*, vol.1 (Chicago and London).

_____. (1974). *The spirit of eastern Christendom (600-1700)*. = *The Christian tradition. A history of the development of doctrine*, vol.2 (Chicago and London).

Pietri, C. (1976). *Roma christiana. Recherches sur l'église de Rome, son organisation, sa politique, son idéologie de Miltiade à Sixte III (311-440)* (Rome).

Pietri, L. (1983). *La ville de Tours du IVe au VIe siècle: naissance d'une cité chrétienne* (Rome).

_____. (1983a). "Les abbés de basilique dans la Gaule du VIe siècle," *Revue d'histoire de l'église de France* 69, pp.5-28.

Prieur, J.-M. (1981). "La figure de l'apôtre dans les Actes apocryphes d'André," in *Les Actes apocryphes des apôtres. Christianisme et monde païen*, ed. F.Bovon et al. (Geneva) 121-39.

Quentin, H. (1921). "La liste des martyrs de Lyon de l'an 177," *Analecta Bollandiana* 39, pp.113-38.

Rice, E.F., Jr. (1985). *Saint Jerome in the Renaissance* (Baltimore and London).

Richards, J. (1979). *The popes and the papacy in the early Middle Ages 476-752* (London).

Riché, P. (1976). *Education and culture in the barbarian West sixth through eighth centuries*, trans. J.J.Contreni (Columbia).

Rouche, M. (1979). *L'Aquitaine des Wisigoths aux Arabes. Naissance d'une région* (Paris).

_____. (1987). "The early Middle Ages in the West," in *A history of private life, 1: From pagan Rome to Byzantium*, ed. P.Veyne, trans. A.Goldhammer (Cambridge, Massachusetts, and London) 411-549.

Sage, M.M. (1975). *Cyprian* (Cambridge, Massachusetts).

Scheibelreiter, G. (1979). "Königstöchter im Kloster. Radegund († 587) und der Nonnenaufstand von Poitiers (589)," *Mitteilungen des Instituts für österreichische Geschichtsforschung* 87, pp.1-37.

Segal, J.B. (1970). *Edessa. 'The blessed city'* (Oxford).

Selle-Hosbach, K. (1974). *Prosopographie merowingischer Amtsträger in der Zeit von 511 bis 613* (Bonn).

van der Straeten, J. (1960). "La Passion de S. Patrocle de Troyes. Ses sources," *Analecta Bollandiana* 78, pp.145-53.

_____. (1978). "Saint Irénée fut-il martyr?" in *Les martyrs de Lyon (177). Lyon, 20-23 septembre 1977* (Paris) 145-52.

Stroheker, K.F. (1948). *Der senatorische Adel im spätantiken Gallien* (Tubingen).

Thompson, E.A. (1969). *The Goths in Spain* (Oxford).

Thorpe, L. (1974), trans. *Gregory of Tours, The history of the Franks* (Harmondsworth).

Van Dam, R. (1985). *Leadership and community in late antique Gaul* (Berkeley).

_____. (forthcoming), trans. *Gregory of Tours, Glory of the confessors* (Liverpool).

Vieillard-Troiekouroff, M. (1976). *Les monuments religieux de la Gaule d'après les oeuvres de Grégoire de Tours* (Paris).

Vikan, G. (1984). "Art, medicine, and magic in early Byzantium," in *Symposium on Byzantine medicine*, ed. J.Scarborough. *Dumbarton Oaks Papers* 38, pp.65-86.

Vollmann, B.K. (1983). "Gregory IV (Gregory von Tours)," in *Reallexikon für Antike und Christentum*, ed. T.Klauser et al., vol.12 (Stuttgart, 1983), col.895-930.

Wallace-Hadrill, J.M. (1967). *The barbarian West 400-1000* (London, 3rd ed.).

_____. (1983). *The Frankish Church* (Oxford).

Weidemann, M. (1982). *Kulturgeschichte der Merowingerzeit nach den Werken Gregors von Tours* (Mainz), 2 vols.

Wemple, S.F. (1981). *Women in Frankish society. Marriage and the cloister 500-900* (Philadelphia).

Wessel, K. (1967). "Der nackte Crucifixus von Narbonne," *Rivista di archeologia cristiana* 43, pp.333-45.

Wickham, C. (1981). *Early medieval Italy. Central power and local society 400-1000* (London).

Wilkinson, J. (1977). *Jerusalem pilgrims before the Crusades* (Warminster).

Wood, I.N. (1979). "Early Merovingian devotion in town and country," in *The Church in town and countryside*, ed. D.Baker. *Studies in Church History* 16 (Oxford) 61-76.

———. (1981). "A prelude to Columbanus: the monastic achievement in the Burgundian territories," in *Columbanus and Merovingian monasticism*, ed. H.B.Clarke and M.Brennan. BAR International Series 113 (Oxford) 3-32.

———. (1983). "The ecclesiastical politics of Merovingian Clermont," in *Ideal and reality in Frankish and Anglo-Saxon society. Studies presented to J.M.Wallace-Hadrill*, ed. P.Wormald, D.Bullough, and R.Collins (Oxford) 34-57.

———. (1985). "Gregory of Tours and Clovis," *Revue belge de philologie et d'histoire* 63, pp.249-72.

———. (1986). "Disputes in late fifth- and sixth-century Gaul: some problems," in *The settlement of disputes in early medieval Europe*, ed. W.Davies and P.Fouracre (Cambridge) 7-22.

———. (forthcoming). "Aspects of the cult of the XL Martyrs in the early medieval West," in *Proceedings of the Belfast conference on the 40 Martyrs*, ed. M.Mullett.

Zelzer, K. (1972). "Zu den lateinischen Fassungen der Thomasakten. 2.Uberlieferung und Sprache," *Wiener Studien* 85, n.s.6, pp.185-212.

———. (1977). "Zur Frage des Autors der Miracula B. Andreae Apostoli und zur Sprache des Gregor von Tours," *Grazer Beiträge* 6, pp.217-41.

INDEX

ASSOCIATION INTERNATIONALE
D'ETUDES PATRISTIQUES
International Association
for Patristic Studies

The Association exists to promote Patristic Studies in various ways. Its chief activity is to compile and publish annually a list of present and future patristic actvity, both in the form of research projects and conferences. It also provides a list of members and their fields of interest.

The purpose of these published Bulletins is to enable scholarship to advance with maximum co-operation and without unnecessary repetition and overlap. It is also envisaged that the discipline itself may be promoted by consultation in various other ways.

For further details please write to:

Professor the Revd. S.G. Hall
Department of Christian Doctrine and History
King's College London (KQC)
Strand
London WC2R 2LS